JonBenét's Mother:
The Tragedy and The Truth!

by Linda Edison McLean

McClain Printing Company
212 Main Street
Parsons, WV 26287
1998
Publishing Division

International Standard Book Number 0-87012-596-6
Library of Congress Catalog Card Number 98-091774
Copyright © 1998 McClain Printing Company
Parsons, West Virginia
Copyright © 1998 Linda McLean
Parkersburg, West Virginia
All Rights Reserved

Forward

by Patsy Ramsey

The important thing about JonBenét is. . .
She was always there for me.
She had golden hair.
She was never mean.
She helped me.
She knew how to treat a friend.
She was generous.
But the important thing about JonBenét is. . .
She was always there for me.

-Quinn Haisley
JonBenét's friend

Of the many cards and letters we have received since JonBenét's death, this poem written by her dearest friend has touched me like no other. For it has been said that if we go through this life knowing the closeness of only one true friendship, then we are indeed blessed. It gives me the purest joy and serenity to know that JonBenét and her little friend shared such a special relationship at a very tender age.

I, too, am blessed to have had a life full of tremendously giving and genuinely caring friends. For what are our lives, really, but a compilation of the experiences and memories shared with friends and family over the years?

In these past months of overwhelming grief and sadness, it has been the undaunted steadfastness of friends and family and a deepening faith in a loving God that have sustained me. Everything else is fleeting–time, material possessions, beauty, health.

I love JonBenét and I miss her so much. My chest physically aches with the pain of a broken heart. I know that anyone who has suddenly lost someone they love understands the emptiness I feel. The heinous crime just adds to the pain. It hurts me to watch my husband and the rest of our family suffer.

Add to that, the helplessness I feel when fingers are pointed and I have to say the words, "I did not kill my baby." Some days it is almost too much to bear. I can force the pain deep inside and go through the motions of living, but the hurt works its way free and overwhelms me again. It is then that I lean on my friends and family for support. I thank God that I have them.

Although I knew that this book was being written, I will read it for the first time as you are. My heartfelt thanks go to all of those who have once again stood by me through the storms of my life. Your support through my battle with cancer was part of what helped make me well. Your willingness to publicly show your faith in me at this tragic time in my life is part of what gives me the strength to face each day.

Genuine friends and a loving family are blessings from above. They are gifts to us that God places in our pathway to be His hands and heart for the short time we are on this earth.

For after all, a wise young poet once said. . .

"The important thing about (friends) is that they are always there for you."

Thank you for being there for me.
Love,
Patsy

for
JonBenét
and for
Jim

this book is dedicated to
all of those who have lost a loved one
too suddenly and too soon

All author profits from the sale of this book
will be donated to the *JonBenét Ramsey Children's Foundation.*

Table of Contents

Introduction:
Enough is Enough!!

On December 26, 1996, JonBenét Ramsey's body was found in the basement of her home. This lovely, innocent little girl had been strangled and beaten. Her parents, John and Patsy, experienced the horror that every parent fears most: their beloved child was gone. Adding to the agony was the devastation of knowing the appalling, evil way that she had been killed. How could they stand the pain? Who could possibly have done this? And why?

But then came even more heartache. The police began to act like they suspected John and Patsy of having something to do with this monstrous crime. At first, even though the suspicion was distressing, John and Patsy understood that the police had to consider any possibilities. But as time went on and the police and media seemed to focus only on them, John and Patsy were not only devastated, but also frustrated and angry. They felt that all of the time spent looking at them was *wasted* time that the authorities could have used to search for the guilty maniac!

Patsy and John's friends and family were outraged. Anyone who knows these wonderful people could not believe that there would be even the slightest doubt of their innocence. But the ridiculous suspicions went on. And the ludicrous publicity got worse. It was like the whole country had become obsessed!

Why write this book now? Because, quite frankly, **I have had enough**. I have heard and watched the innuendoes, false statements, interviews-for-money, misinformed and misleading segments, incredible tabloid trash, and all of the other untruths which have been "reported" about two wonderful human beings. And it's time to speak the truth.

Why haven't the Ramseys' friends and family spoken out sooner? Mainly, we have respected their right to privacy. We didn't think it was right to talk publicly about such a painful, personal matter. So we have all remained in silent support- -waiting and hoping that somehow the truth would come out and Patsy and John would no longer have to suffer. It doesn't seem to be happening that way. And we can no longer stand silent.

Another reason that I personally haven't spoken out is that, like most people, I'm very shy of the media. I have been called by everyone from *People Magazine* to the *National Enquirer*. A reporter from *Hard Copy* walked into my office and *Geraldo Rivera's* producer offered to fly me to New York so I could tell my story. But I am just a small-town mom who couldn't imagine getting involved with all of that. I would be nervous in front of a camera. I would be sorry if I would say anything that could be misinterpreted or edited to be out of context. And I know if I had to face people who were accusing Patsy that I would be so angry I might have an embarrassing outburst.

But it's gone too far now. I don't buy the tabloids but I see the headlines when I am in the line at the grocery store. They are ludicrous. I've seen everything from "Proof That Mom did It" to "Proof That Dad Did It" to "9-Year Old Brother Did It". I expect them soon to write: "Proof That Alien Abductors Did It". The stories that are run in those scandal-papers are so ridiculous that I really don't want to think that anyone could possibly believe them. But when I saw the editor of one of these tabloids on a so-called "reputable" television show, it made me shiver. Surely, honest, intelligent Americans know when they are being sold lies for profit!

It's like a hunt where the snarling dogs (tabloids) chase the poor fox until it drops. The fox can't fight back–it's tired and scared and certainly has done nothing to deserve the attack. But even worse than the mindless dogs are the hunters (mainstream press) who sit on their high-horse and trail along behind--shouting for blood. And many people sadly seem to enjoy the spectacle of the hunt, watching the pack of dogs on their feeding frenzy. They are buying the trash, watching the dirt and believing it as the truth. *I want us to be better people than that!*

The media always seem to find people who want to talk

X

about a tragedy (usually for money). And the more negative they are, the more publicity they seem to get. The night I decided I really wanted to do something was the night I saw a so-called "close friend/photographer" of Patsy's being interviewed. She talked about Patsy not crying when she last saw her--implying, I guess, that if you don't cry every minute, then you aren't suffering. I thought, *Why is she on there? Why is she doing that?* I knew how Patsy had cried and I knew that her pain was real. This media frenzy has led to betrayals and suspicions and made a tragic situation even worse.

I can't believe that this has become such an obsession. It seems we have forgotten that real people are involved--*people who have feelings.* Some of those in the media act like the public has a right to know every detail of people's lives and if people ask for privacy, they must be guilty of something. I get so angry that I find myself wanting to yell at people on the television screen, *"Why can't you just leave them alone with their grief?"*

And the internet! I knew there were things online so just before I finished this book, I took a closer look. Unbelievable! There are websites that are devoted exclusively to JonBenét's murder. Again, I just can't understand this obsession. Most of the pages are negative and one-sided. Some are so unfair--and so untrue. There are "doctored" photos. There are chat rooms (like some radio talk shows) where people write mean, hateful, vindictive things about people they have never met. Online or on the air, they can say whatever they want because they can remain anonymous. It makes me very afraid that our children will grow up with access to these and other such lies and distortions and that the authors don't have to answer to anyone for slander or libel. I did find one site (called jameson TimeLine) that seemed like the author(s) believe in the Ramseys' innocence--or at least are willing to look at both sides. But it was the exception. The internet may become the next venue for "lynching" innocents. I just don't understand how a person with any feelings could be a part of this.

We're the Perry Mason/Matlock generation. We watch the law shows on television and they always find the killer before the end of the program. We want a quick solution. Usually Mason and Matlock, as lawyers for the defense, not only clear their client but discover the guilty party. It's in a nice, neat little hour-long package and the good guys win.

But it doesn't happen so easily in real life. Sometimes innocent people get accused (ask Richard Jewell) and we are all willing to accept whatever the media feeds us. Sometimes the truth may never be found. But we don't like it that way! We want an answer! And so we are willing to place the blame wherever we are told. But are we willing to look at the other side?

Some people think because this book contains *good things* about *good people* that it will not be read. I hope that isn't so. I hope our appetites have not been so trained to savor the trash that we will not be willing to taste the truth. I had a literary agent tell me that I should sell this story to the tabloids--that's the place this story belongs. I sure hope he's wrong. If the public will not look at the other side and continues to believe only the lies, then I have lost my faith in the American sense of fair play!

I once asked Patsy, as she sat across from me at my kitchen table, *"Doesn't it bother you that these things are said, that these lies are spread?"*

Her answer was given slowly and with obvious pain, *"I am so far down and they have kicked me so hard that I really don't care anymore. They can keep on kicking and they can't hurt me worse than I have already been hurt."*

Patsy called me at my office on the Tuesday before Thanksgiving, 1997 to see how I was doing. I told her I was having a rough time since this was the first time my children and I were going to celebrate Thanksgiving at home since my husband Jim had died of cancer. She said she expected it to be just like any other day for her. *"I miss JonBenét so much that every day is hard and I can't imagine one day being harder than another."* (Later that day, a wonderful Thanksgiving flower arrangement was delivered to me at work. It was from Patsy; she was thinking of someone else's pain.)

I had already talked to Patsy about the idea of some of her friends finally speaking up to show how much we believe in her. She had said she'd think about it. When I called to thank her for the flowers, I told her about my "enough is enough" feeling. I told her I wanted to write this book. She said something like, *"Thanks for caring so much; maybe it is time for people to say what they feel. Go ahead and do whatever you want."*

One of the things that influenced my decision was when

I saw a friend of John's named Jim Marino on a television show the night before Patsy's call. Jim is a long-time friend of John Ramsey's and he had decided that he wanted to speak up for his friend. You could tell that he sincerely believed in John. But Jim had to admit he doesn't know Patsy very well.

I, on the other hand, have known Patsy for twenty-five years and I decided if Jim Marino could speak out, maybe I should, too. I could tell by Jim's interview that he was nervous and didn't particularly enjoy the attention. But I guess he, too, had decided: "**Enough is enough!**"

My part of this book is mostly about Patsy because I don't know John Ramsey as well. I have talked with him at length though, about how frustrating and painful this ordeal has been. I have to say that I like him a lot. His sincerity and goodness are apparent even to someone who isn't a very close friend. I do know that Patsy's family loves him and trusts him. Many of Patsy's friends who wrote in this book are also good friends of John. And they all have wonderful things to say about him, as you will read.

Every penny of the writer's profit on this book will be donated to the JonBenét Ramsey Children's Foundation. This foundation has been formed to create a legacy for JonBenét. It is important to her parents and family and friends that she will not have died in vain. It is important that something will be accomplished in her name that will help other children. If ever there were a circumstance to test a person's faith, this is it. But we will maintain our faith and we will find a way to make JonBenét Ramsey proud of us as the Foundation tries to make good things happen in the name of this little angel.

Why have we written this book? Because we are tired of the false accusations. Because we are angry with the lies. Because we are frustrated with the way the case has been handled.

We are a variety of people of different ages from different parts of the country who are coming together with one common bond: **We believe in Patsy and John Ramsey with all our hearts**. We have faith in human reason. We have faith in normal people. We believe that when you get to know Patsy and John you will realize how wonderful they are. You will know in your heart that this father did not murder his little girl. You will know in your soul that this mother did not kill her baby.

Chapter One:
Patsy's High School Years

I first met Patsy Paugh in 1973. I was the rookie coach of the Parkersburg, West Virginia, High School speech and debate team; she was a high school junior with the personality, dedication, talent and leadership that any coach dreams of. It was kind of like a first-year football coach finding an All-American quarterback on the team.

When I began teaching, I was in my mid-20s, just a few years older than some of my students. Because I was so young and energetic, I was naively confident that I could handle anything. I not only taught several different courses of English, speech and debate but I volunteered to coach the forensics teams and to direct the senior play. I was in for some terrific but very challenging times. I had the advantage of a great student-teacher and some experienced speech team members who helped guide their new coach. Also, I had some very talented and dedicated first-year team members like Patsy. I'm sure this fantastic group of kids would have won with or without me as their coach. But win they did!

It's been years since I have taught, but the memories came back to me in the summer of 1997, when one of the Ramseys' private investigators came to meet with me. Unlike the police detectives who only asked for handwriting samples, he asked me to get out any yearbooks, scrapbooks, pictures, etc. that I could find which dealt with Patsy. I only taught at PHS for five years before I quit to have my first child, so all of my old "memories" from teaching were in one plastic storage box. I have high school yearbooks from each year, an old scrapbook with yellowed newspaper articles about our speech/debate program and a bag of memorabilia from the Miss America Pageants that I attended with Patsy and later with her sister Pam.

The first speech tournament that I have a record that

we attended was held at Marshall University in Huntington, West Virginia. The article doesn't give a date, but it does list the winners from our school. Patsy won a first place and a second place trophy at that first tournament and she went on to win several other honors throughout the year. At the state tournament held at West Virginia Wesleyan College in the spring, PHS placed first from among thirty-two schools entered. Patsy was selected as the winner in the oral interpretation category. I have one particular picture that makes me smile even today. It's of Patsy accepting the team trophy from the President of Wesleyan, Jay Rockefeller. (He went on to become the governor of West Virginia and is now the state's senator.) She looked so happy--so typical of a high school student who has just won something we had practiced for months to achieve. It still makes me smile to see the expression on her face (*see photo*).

Patsy was always well-prepared and liked to win as much as anyone. But she also helped others, willing to do anything to spark the team spirit. And her family was always there to help. Whether we needed cookies for a late night practice or transportation to a tournament across the state, I could always count on the Paughs.

Along with the other PHS state-champion, Patsy represented West Virginia in the National Forensics Tournament in Dallas. As with most "non-sports" high school activities, we had to raise the money ourselves to attend the nationals, but it was worth it. I was grateful to these students for having the talent that made it possible for me to attend the national championships my very first year of coaching. I gained experience and knowledge so I could better help our teams in the coming years. Patsy later told me she especially remembered that trip because it was her first time on an airplane. She didn't place in the finals that year, but we had a great time at Southern Methodist University!

Patsy's senior year was pretty much like her junior year--only busier. She continued to compete in speech tournaments along with her other activities. From what I could tell, her other teachers thought as much of her as I did. She was one of the most well-rounded students I ever taught. The 1975 yearbook list of Patsy's high school activities includes: "Elks Leadership, Junior Orchesis (dance group), Junior Varsity Cheerleader, Masque & Gavel (Speech/Debate honorary), Pep Club, Red Wing

Drill Team, Student-Faculty Forum, Teenager of the Month, VFW Voice of Democracy district winner and more."

The forensics team won the state championship that year, too, though I don't think Patsy placed first in her category. We did enter a competition sponsored by the National Catholic Forensics League and Patsy won the right to attend their national tournament in Philadelphia. She placed second in those national finals which was the highest any member of my teams ever placed. Patsy worked very hard and deserved the honor. Patsy wasn't a "natural" talent. She didn't compete in the categories of extemporaneous or impromptu speaking (where you have to think of things on the spur of the moment.) She liked to meticulously prepare for each competition. She never minded going over and over her presentation. It was this dedication and commitment that I remember most. She wasn't overly concerned about winning, but she wanted to do her very best. And we all enjoyed the victories.

Patsy's mom was a great help to me. Some have wondered if she did too much, but she gave the kind of support that many parents of successful youngsters give. I watch the band team parents who raise money to send their children to march in bowl game parades and the swim team parents who sit on the bleachers all day to see one race. That's what parents do. I have spent many a soggy Saturday afternoon in cold, rainy weather watching my sons play soccer in the mud. Patsy's mom certainly didn't go as far as the gymnastics parents who agree to let their daughter live with a coach in another state or ice skating parents who are at the rink by 5:30 a.m. to get practice time. We sing the praises of Tiger Woods' father who coached his son to achieve his dream. He is a good man and he produced a good son who worked hard from the time he was very, very young to become the best in his sport. And we admire that parental support. It's no different with Little League dads or cheerleader moms. It's a great thing to support our children in their chosen activities. It only is bad when it goes too far--when the parent or child is unfair to others or the parent pushes the child farther than the child wants to go. It was definitely not this way with Patsy's mom. She was just a very supportive mother hen and, now that I have children, I appreciate her even more.

I've heard media talk about Patsy's support of JonBenét's pageant experiences as if that were a crime. I don't understand what people find so strange. JonBenét liked this activity. Patsy was the same with JonBenét as she was with her other children--the same as her parents had been with her. She made a variety of activities available for them and supported them in the ones they liked best. She didn't push; she didn't force; she just was a mom. But we will look at that issue in the chapter about Patsy as a mother.

The other students in her high school class appreciated Patsy for her sincerity and goodness. They had a large graduating class. Patsy was chosen by her classmates as one of four students to address the class at commencement. That was an honor. It showed how much her peers thought of her because they wanted her to speak at their graduation. One of the other three speakers that year was Diane (Dunn) McClure.

Here are some thoughts from Diane:

"Patsy, or 'P' as I call her, is one of my oldest and best friends. She was one of the first people I met when I moved to West Virginia in 1969. I was moving in my seventh grade year which was completely devastating for me, but thanks to Patsy and the other neighborhood girls, I was happy within a very short time in my new home. We had a wonderful time "hanging out"--taking turns with the weekend slumber parties and other typical seventh-grade activities.

"I admired Patsy from the start because she loved to try everything. I sort of attached myself to her coattails and I ended up having the best junior and senior high school years anyone could ask for. We did cheerleading together, band and drill team together and danced in talent shows together. In fact, one of my funniest memories is Patsy and I doing a Mexican tap dance with sombreros on our heads that seemed bigger than we were. She had a way of encouraging me to do more than I ever thought I could. Even if I didn't have the experience or talent, she gave me the confidence to try. The day we both gave speeches to our senior class at graduation was one of the proudest days of my life.

"One of Patsy's biggest strengths was her family. I know that one of the only ways she is getting through this tragedy is with the help of her family and the faith they gave her in her early years. Patsy set goals, studied and worked hard. To be hon-

4

est, I was more focused on having a good time and the education part came second. Patsy was always extra special. She was the straight arrow. But we were a good pair and remained close friends. We never judged each other on our differences; we always knew we could count on each other. We were college roommates for three years, were part of each other's wedding days and have kept in contact ever since. We shared each other's thoughts and dreams and I know to this day I could count on her for anything. And I would do anything for her!

"I just can't believe this has happened to her. No one should have to endure this nightmare, especially not her--the girl who never did the wrong thing. Patsy is a great mom! When we were fortunate enough to get together with our kids, she always showed how much she loved her children and how proud she was of them. She has been proud of John and what he accomplished and she felt she was a part of those accomplishments. But her children were her life.

"When Patsy got cancer, we couldn't believe it. Not Patsy! Not someone so good! She fought it so hard and I was so proud of her and I admired her strength. She fought the cancer for her kids and for John and she fought it with her faith. Now she has an even harder battle and I hope she can find the faith to fight just as hard to overcome this--but I don't know how.

"I think in my heart that people would probably not be questioning Patsy and John if it were not for Susan Smith's murder of her two sons. That story destroyed our trust in her as a mother and we were betrayed by her plea of innocence. But I am here to shout that Patsy is not that mother! She is not capable of anything like this! She is a good, warm, kind person--the very best! We all love her. And P, we always have been and always will be here for you!"

signed: Diane Dunn McClure

Patsy filled a whole page in the back of my 1975 yearbook. As anyone who has been a teacher will tell you, it means so much when a student takes the time and effort to express feelings like this. It makes a teacher's job worthwhile to know that your "children" think nice things, but students don't often take the time to say them. I am going to include her words here, not to inflate my ego, but to show you what a considerate person she was--even at that young age. She wrote in May of 1975:

> *"Mrs. McLean,*
> *What can I say--where do I begin to tell you how much my two years in Speech have meant to me and how much you mean to me. I have had so many beautiful, rewarding and memorable experiences over these past two years that I can't even begin to count them all. I'll never forget Dallas, my first plane trip, the Bar-B-Q and Six Flags. That was the best summer I've ever had-really-and it wouldn't--couldn't have been possible without your 'get up and go!'*
> *This year has been great--I guess you're right--there will probably never be a year like this one! There is so much I want to say but I can't find the words to say it. I just want you to know that you've been more--much more--than a 'teacher'--you've been a friend and a dear one. And it won't end here. I'll probably be talking to you a lot about a lot of things before it's over. (When you do finally decide to have kids--call me--I want to be one of the first to know!!)*
> *We'll I'm taking too much room, so I'll end by saying that I love you and I wish you all the happiness in the world. (You've already got your 'hubby' so you're halfway there!) Remember me like I'll remember you. . .Bye now! Patsy"*

That was a condensed look at Patsy in high school where I first met her. What does all of this have to do with the tragic loss of her daughter? This is just chapter one of a life where no one can find any "deep dark secrets". She was not an embittered high school outcast. She didn't have family problems or self-esteem problems or personality problems. She was as "typical" as you could find. Perhaps she had a little more success than most, but she was just a pretty, perky, talented, nice high school student that any parent would be proud of--that any teacher would be glad to have--that any student would be happy to call a friend.

And the rest of her life would follow this pattern. But before we move on, let's take a look at Patsy's childhood before I met her.

Patsy's high school yearbook senior picture.

Patsy as 1975 winner of "Voice of Democracy" contest.

Jay Rockefeller, president of West Virginia Wesleyan College presenting first prize for Parkersburg High School as winners of state speech tournament. Patsy accepting on behalf of team.

Patsy's first pageant. DeMolay
Sweetheart 1972. She was fifteen
years old.

DALLAS BOUND-Dave Warfield, *left*, president of the Parkersburg Lions Club, presents a $100 check to Mrs. Linda McLean and her speech students, to be applied towards the fund to send them to the National Forensics Tournament in Dallas.

Patsy Paugh practices for trip to Dallas, TX for National Speech Tournament.

Friend Diane Dunn says Patsy was her inspiration to enter into activities that she might have been too shy to join on her own.

Chapter Two:
Patsy's Childhood

Patricia Ann Paugh was born on December 29, 1956, in St. Joseph's Hospital in Parkersburg, West Virginia. She weighed five pounds and five ounces and was nineteen inches long. Patsy, as she was nicknamed, was the first of three daughters born to Don and Nedra Paugh.

Nedra was the youngest of six Rymer children. She was very close to her sister Naomi, who was three years older. The girls were both cheerleaders and would often have their "beaus" over to the house to play cards. Nedra met Don Paugh when they were in high school. They were both from Ritchie County, West Virginia, and would sometimes drive all the way into Wood County to visit the "big city" of Parkersburg to go to the movies or dance to the big bands.

After Don and Nedra were married and Don had graduated from West Virginia University with a degree in engineering, they moved to Parkersburg and lived in a little apartment near the bakery. Nedra had a degree from the local business college and was hired as secretary to the bakery owner. His daughter, Susan, remembers well how wonderful Mrs. Paugh was to her.

"I looked forward to going to daddy's office after school. Nedra was his secretary and she would give me little tasks to do to 'help.' She set up a card table so I could put daily reports in order and staple them. Each week, she gave me a little manila envelope with my pay (in quarters).

"But Nedra did more for me than just play games. She was so kind and acted genuinely glad to see me. She didn't treat me like a bother or like I was in the way. I thought she was so pretty and yet she treated me special--and she complimented me!

She always told me what a good job I was doing and encouraged me to think I was capable. I realize now how much she helped this shy little girl with my self-esteem. I wanted to be just like her when I grew up! (Note: Susan did grow up to be a business woman, taking over as president of the bakery when her father died.)

"When I heard about JonBenét's death, my first thought was for Nedra. I knew she was suffering. I wanted so much to help but I knew there wasn't much I could do. I later read a magazine article which said unfair, unkind things about Nedra. It hurt me and it offended me that, for no good reason, they would print things that hurt innocent people. I was surprised at how strong my feelings were for someone I had known so long ago. I realized how much she still meant to me. She was a very strong influence on my life.

"I recently had lunch with Nedra. She worries about her daughter and wishes Patsy could rest more. She talked about John lovingly, as though he were a son, not just a son-in-law. We remembered how it was over 40 years ago and wondered why things had to happen as they do. Her hands were gnarled from arthritis but she still had that beautiful smile that I remembered so well. I cried for her, for all that she has had to face and for what is yet to come.

"I realize that part of the reason I feel so deeply is that I have also recently lost a child; my son died two years ago. I understand how, as a grieving parent, you often lapse into tears but then you remember something that makes you smile. The ups and downs, the questions and the pain come and go seemingly at will. I know what it is like to go through stages of grief and to feel sorrow and anger and emptiness. But it's beyond my comprehension to think that the media would hound the Ramseys and the Paughs during their grief. It's beyond my understanding how reporters can attack and try to destroy other members of the family. I know in my heart that they are wonderful people and I send them my prayers."

signed: Susan Storck Ross

While Nedra worked in the office, Don Paugh took a job with Bendix Westinghouse. They set up housekeeping and they planned a family. In the meantime, Nedra enjoyed sister Naomi's three sons: Tom, Greg and Randy. Naomi didn't drive so Nedra helped by taking them to the circus, Boy Scout meetings, etc.

Just after Nedra learned she was going to have her first child, sister Naomi found out that she was going to have her fourth child. Just two and half months after Patsy was born, her first cousin Debra Diane Shepler was born on March 14, 1957.

From the beginning, Debbie and Patsy were more than cousins, they were like sisters. And it wasn't just their relationship that was close; it was their physical appearance. Even today, it is uncanny how much they look alike (*see color photo 1*). Their size, their facial expressions, even their voices are surprisingly similar. Each is petite with beautiful dark hair and a dazzling friendly smile that makes you want to smile back. Their big eyes are striking; both had blue eyes growing up--which later turned to a shade of green. Debbie says they often find they even have the same taste, like choosing the identical wallpaper pattern or picking out the same outfit of clothes while shopping.

Here is Cousin Debbie's story:

"I don't remember everything about the early years of my life. I do remember how much my cousins were a part of my childhood. Probably because I had 3 older brothers, I seemed to spend a lot of time with Patsy (and later her 2 sisters). Aunt Nedra would include me in the 'girl times'. I remember going with them to see Walt Disney movies; I especially remember how much we loved Mary Poppins.

"I sometimes went to Sunday school with Patsy at Stout Memorial Church and I remember being so proud of the art projects that we'd make in class. Aunt Nedra gave all 4 of us girls 'school days' memory books with our names on them and little white Bibles; I still have mine. Patsy has always been very religious. Grandma Rymer was a big influence on her children and grandchildren. She always told us that God is in our hearts and I remember her saying 'if you ever have a problem, turn to Jesus.' Patsy passed along her love of God to her children and JonBenét seemed to understand, even at her young age. Evening prayers were a family tradition--generation after generation. I remember the prayer we said most often was 'Now I lay me down to sleep' and Patsy probably taught that one to JonBenét, too.

17

How tragic the words: 'If I should die before I wake, I pray the Lord my soul to take.'

"I remember how much I liked to visit Uncle Don's family in the country. We'd play wiffle ball and rock in the big glider on the front porch. We did so many family things together that they just called us 'the Paugh girls'. The first time I ever realized how much we looked alike was a day we were in the dime store downtown and a lady asked us if we were twins. We sure laughed about that one! There have been times in our lives when we resembled each other a lot and times when I don't think we did. I wore glasses; Patsy didn't. Patsy wore braces; I didn't. But people tell me now that we look more and more alike all of the time. I consider that a real compliment! They say we looked like our Grandma Rymer (see photo).

"The main thing about our childhood is that it was so ordinary. The things we did were normal little girl things. Their dog, Cinder, was a puppy of our dog, Mitzi. I spent the night at their house a lot. We giggled and did each other's hair and played with makeup. We took ballet and tap dancing lessons together. At one recital, Patsy and I were supposed to lead the rest of the group onto the stage. Patsy took off and did exactly what she had practiced; I stood back and cried. I guess from the beginning, Patsy was a leader and not afraid to be in front of a crowd.

"Patsy liked dancing. Her sister Pam loved to sing. The youngest, Paulette (Polly) played the flute. Each girl had her own talent and Aunt Nedra and Uncle Don supported each in whatever she attempted. But I was there and I know that my cousins weren't pushed into anything they didn't want to do.

"We often spent Christmas together. Grandma and Grandpa Rymer had moved to Parkersburg and we would play "grocery store" in their basement. We had a little cash register and made up silly skits. When I think about our childhood, all sorts of unrelated wonderful memories come into my head: riding bicycles, roller skating, playing pin-the-tail-on-the-donkey at each other's birthday parties, playing with Barbie dolls, watching Polly's swim meets, catching lightning bugs. (We let them go because we couldn't stand to see them die.) My mom and dad considered Patsy as much a part of our family as Patsy's family did me. We had such good times together; the memories still make me smile.

"I remember that as we got older, we liked to play rock 'n

roll records. Patsy's family had a jukebox in the basement and we would do the "Twist" and the "Pony". Patsy, Pam and I would imitate the Supremes and sing along with the Beatles.

"Patsy and I were not in the same activities in high school. She was on the field at the football games performing as a member of the Red Wings Drill Team; I was sitting in the stands with the Pep Club. But we were always together at family gatherings and were always there for each other when we needed to talk. We both graduated from Parkersburg High School in 1975 and we both left for West Virginia University in the fall. We pledged different sororities; Patsy majored in journalism and my degree is in social work. But we saw each other fairly often and it sure was nice to know we had 'family' while we were away from home for the first time.

"Marriage, children, careers, and moving would separate us after college. But I will always cherish our childhood together and consider Patsy the sister I never had. Our paths have crossed in many ways throughout our lives and I will have more to say in later chapters. But this I have to say right now:

"Patsy and I are a lot alike in our personalities, sort of easy going and patient. I don't recall us ever having an argument. But I think Patsy was a better person than I was--she still is. Even as a child and a teenager, she was fair and generous and loving with everyone she met. She didn't get angry--or gossip--or hold a grudge--or wish ill to anyone. Everyone liked Patsy because she was just plain good! And she's the same today as she was then.

"I'm not saying this just because of the book. I am repeating what I have said many, many times: Patsy is the best and kindest person I have ever known."

signed: Debbie Shepler Krieg

It was heartwarming for me to talk with Patsy's cousin Debbie. I had met her in the past--most recently at JonBenét's funeral. But our lengthy and candid talk made us both realize that we weren't alone in our overpowering belief in Patsy's goodness. And I would find many, many others who shared our belief.

Another of the people who has known Patsy from the time she was very young is Judy (Mason) Schoch. She was proud to tell of her strong feelings of support for her lifelong friend.

Here is Judy's story:

"I first met Patsy (I have called her 'P-Paugh' for as long as I can remember) in the fourth grade at Emerson Elementary School in Parkersburg. I had transferred from another grade school and I remember being apprehensive about a new place. Patsy was so warm and friendly that we hit it off right away. We became fast friends and for a long time we spent many of our weekends roller skating at the local roller rink. We had so much fun (and I remember us becoming pretty good skaters--at least we thought so!)

"We didn't attend the same junior high but hooked up again our sophomore year at Parkersburg High School and we were both on the school drill team. Patsy was in so many activities that I was amazed at how she found time for it all. She really seemed to enjoy all that she did. Somehow she managed to be active in many things, do well in school academically and still be a nice person. She treated everyone the same--there was nothing not to like about P-Paugh.

"After we graduated, we both went to West Virginia University and joined the Alpha Xi Delta sorority and thus were together for 4 more years. We had some great times in college. I remember being so happy for Patsy when she won Miss West Virginia. Patsy enjoyed the pageants and worked hard. I respected her for it and remember feeling how much she deserved to win. I told Patsy that I wasn't surprised--I knew she was destined for big things in life! On occasion, I would catch a ride home from WVU with Patsy in her official Miss West Virginia car. What fun we had! And she wasn't the least bit stuck up about it. She was just plain old P-Paugh.

"After college, we both moved away and married. We kept in touch about the births of our babies and saw each other at class reunions. I was devastated when I learned of Patsy's ovarian cancer. My beloved mother died of cancer at a young age and this is one particular disease that I loathe. I got some beautiful letters from Patsy during her illness. She was so strong, both physically and mentally, and her faith in God was so deep that I knew if anyone could beat this disease, it would be her. I was thrilled when I heard she was 'cured'.

"We last saw each other at our twenty-year reunion in 1995 (see photo). She looked radiant and the picture of health.

We sat together all evening and had a grand time. I remember telling my husband that P-Paugh was the same as she'd always been: nice, sweet and a little corny. She loved to laugh. She told me she had taken John, Burke and JonBenét to our old elementary school and sat in some of our old classrooms (see photo). Patsy has always seemed to cherish her roots. I guess maybe it was even more apparent after she was so close to death.

"The day my brother called to tell me of JonBenét's death was horrible. I was in shock--it couldn't be! Nothing has affected me so terribly except my own mother's death. When JonBenét died, my oldest daughter was in fourth grade--the same age Patsy and I were when we first met and became friends. For some reason I remember going to see The Sound of Music with Patsy and her mother, many years ago. My girls love this movie and the songs in it. How ironic. Patsy did 'follow her rainbow and find her dream' and then someone destroyed it.

"It is agony to see a friend of yours go through something like this--to deal with such a tragedy and then all of the publicity. . .people talking, accusing, drawing their own conclusions without knowing the facts. I hate to go to the grocery store because of the junk printed about the Ramseys. I hope P-Paugh feels my thoughts and prayers--that's all I can give her at this time. Except that I can publicly proclaim my absolute faith in the wonderful little girl, the loyal high school teammate, the college sister, the faithful cancer survivor and the terrific mother that I know as my friend P-Paugh!"

signed: Judy Mason Schoch

So we find no "deep dark secrets" in Patsy's childhood, no nagging problems or hidden scars that could be used to imply something sinister. We find just a loving and normal childhood--perhaps as much of an American dream as ever there was.

Now that you've met Patsy as I first knew her during her high school years and we've flashed back to her childhood, let's look at another chapter of her life. Let's look at how Patsy went from high school standout to college graduate--with a stop along the way to become Miss West Virginia.

Don and Nedra Paugh--Wedding Day, May 28, 1955.

Patsy, May 1960.

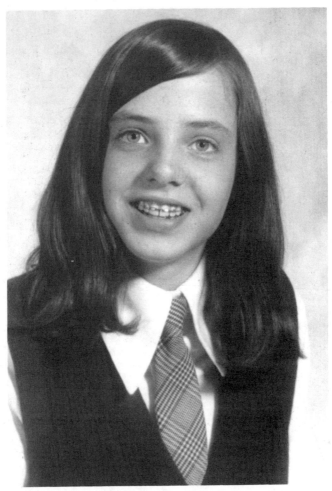

Patsy in seventh grade.

Judy Mason Schoch and Patsy at Parkersburg City Park during twentieth high school reunion, September 1995, with their children.

John, Patsy, JonBenét and Burke. Patsy took them to visit her old elementary school when they came back to Parkersburg for her high school reunion, 1995.

March 31, 1990, Grandma Fay Rymer's 90th birthday. Ken and Naomi Shepler, Fay Rymer, Don and Nedra Paugh.

Chapter Three:
Miss West Virginia

I didn't see Patsy too often during her first year of college. I did run into her from time to time because her sister Pam was a member of our speech team. Pam and Mrs. Paugh would keep me up-to-date on Patsy's college life. She was majoring in journalism, had joined a sorority and was enjoying college life as she had enjoyed every stage of her life thus far.

Patsy won the Miss West Virginia pageant held in June 1977. She had just finished her last final exam of the semester and had to hurry home just in time for the event. For her talent presentation, she used a scene from a play called, "The Prime of Miss Jean Brodie." This was the same scene she had performed to win national honors on our high school forensics team. In oral interpretation, a student takes a scene from a story or play and interprets it for the audience. There are no costumes, props or theatrical makeup and the speaker talks in a different voice for each character.

Patsy had a great personality, but got a little nervous when the spotlight was on. However, she was always willing to work hard and the night of the Miss West Virginia Pageant, that preparation paid off. It's not often that an oral interpretation talent can win over singing or dancing or piano playing (which are more accepted talents). But Patsy's wonderful personality was so evident when she walked onto the stage that you couldn't help but feel you wanted her to represent your state.

After she won the state contest, she asked if I would help her get ready for the Miss America Pageant which was to be held in September in Atlantic City. Although I had never been involved with pageants before, I thought it would be a great experience. When she was preparing for the Miss America pageant, we studied current events. I would pretend to be a judge asking her questions so she could practice her interview answers.

In order to perform her talent selection at the nationally-televised Miss America event, she had to get written permission from certain people. I think it was the author of the novel, the playwright and the studio that produced the movie. But she was denied permission from one of the authors. I don't remember the exact circumstances, but it was a real blow! Under pressure from pageant officials to make a decision by a certain date, Patsy turned to West Virginia's Governor, Jay Rockefeller. Interestingly, he had been president of West Virginia Wesleyan College when Patsy had won first place in the high school state speech contest and he had presented her with her trophy. He worked hard to help her and I think he eventually did get permission, but it came too late.

We waited up until the last possible moment, but when permission had not been granted, Patsy called pageant officials and changed her talent presentation to a dramatic dialogue called "Deadline" which she had been working on writing since the controversy began. It took many hours to write and edit. It wasn't an entire play; it was just one "scene" that had the same types of characters that were in the scene from the play she had used before. She had worked so hard on those characterizations that she just wanted to be able to use the same "voices" and the same "gestures" and the same "emotions" that she had practiced.

Anyway, the scene was between a columnist and a young school teacher and expressed Patsy's views on censorship. I'm not sure if the idea came from her journalism major in college, but I think it probably did. I don't remember the words of the scene at all. I looked for a copy of it but can't find it anywhere. I wonder if they have it on tape at pageant headquarters somewhere. (Isn't it ironic that Patsy then protested censorship and now the tabloid press is using its "freedom" to lie and distort the facts and falsely accuse her!)

We spent the summer of 1977 modifying and rehearsing the two-minute fifty-second piece. She was at our house almost every day. Since I was only eight years older than she was, we became more than teacher and student; as I helped her prepare for the Miss America pageant, we became friends.

I remember when Patsy and my best friend Karen Kincheloe and I went to Columbus to look for outfits for Patsy to wear for the pageant. We spent the day looking for gowns and bathing suits--none of us knowing what colors looked good on television, what styles would compliment her best or anything else about it. But we had a good time and it was one of those experiences that you remember for a long time. Luckily, she had others in the pageant committee who helped her with dresses and I stuck to the talent rehearsals.

They held a fashion show in the meeting hall of Patsy's church the week before we left for Atlantic City. Again, my memory fails, but I do have the newspaper article. It says that she modeled her evening gowns, swimsuit and jeans outfit. The jeans outfit must have been something to represent our state because the report describes it as "featuring the colors of West Virginia with a bright gold jacket, jeans with gold trim and a patch on the back which reads Wild, Wonderful West Virginia."

She also performed for the first time the dramatic dialogue that she would be performing in Atlantic City. Wow! How young and optimistic we must have been. Can you imagine performing something for the first time in public and then a week later performing it for a national audience?

The fashion show got a big write-up in the local paper. That's one of the nice things about being from a place like Parkersburg. Everyone is behind someone who represents their city. It's small town America and the American dream. We were so proud of "our" Patsy.

And she made us proud. I went with Patsy and her family and her official chaperone to Atlantic City for the Miss America Pageant. When I first saw what was called the "Cow Palace," I couldn't get over how *big* it was. Patsy was a little shaky and I couldn't blame her. This was no high school auditorium. This was much more than we'd bargained for. I remember that we then went downstairs into the ballroom of our hotel and she practiced her scene, with me at one end of the ballroom and Patsy at the other so she could "project" her lines much louder than she ever had before. Boy, was I nervous! And I'm sure she was even more so.

When it came time for her performance during the talent section of the preliminary round, I spent the time in the powder room; I just couldn't watch. I had never watched one of my students compete in a final round. But she must have done a good job.

Patsy didn't get in the ten semi-finalists, but she did win a Grand Talent Award and a $2000 scholarship. I personally think she was given this award not only for her special talent, but for her special personality which even the judges had sensed. She wasn't tall enough; she was pretty but not breathtakingly beautiful; she didn't have a talent that could be showcased; she didn't have the most outstanding clothes; she may not have had as much poise and experience as Miss Texas. But she had *something special* and the judges saw it. She was as unpretentious and real as anyone you could meet. I think you can tell when someone is genuine, when her smile is sincere, when her heart is generous. That's what everyone who meets her thinks of Patsy. It's so trite, but so true in her case: she is even more beautiful on the inside than on the outside.

I had never been involved with any pageants before; I was just there to support Patsy, so I'm not any kind of credible source for what goes on at the pageants. But I do know that she was never one to complain, bad-mouth others, pout or act disappointed. Of course she wanted to win, but she wasn't aggressively competitive. She was just a kid having the time of her life and glad to be there. And I was glad to be there with her. It's another life-long memory to cherish.

Patsy's official chaperone was Betty Smith. Betty and her husband Jim had been involved with the pageants for years. They were a real help to the contestants-- "their girls"-- and Patsy has always had wonderful things to say about them. Betty recently wrote me a note:

"All the years we have known Patsy, she has been one of the kindest and most generous persons we know. She came to visit me when I was sick and brought me a gown and housecoat--she remembered my favorite color was blue. She has been generous with support of the pageant and gives a scholarship each year to one of the contestants. For the 50th anniversary of the Miss West Virginia pageant, Patsy and another former winner brought favors and gifts for all of the contestants. Patsy paid for a reception for pageant personnel and guests. I do not know anyone who doesn't admire or like her. . .You know how much we love Patsy and know for sure she had nothing to do with the

murder."

signed: Betty Smith

Again we see Patsy always using what she has to help others.

I traveled with Patsy around the state a little during her year as Miss West Virginia. We would take off in her yellow Oldsmobile (provided by the local car dealer where my husband worked) with her "Miss West Virginia" seal on the door. And the truckers would honk and the little kids would wave. Patsy would cut ribbons and make little speeches. And the people loved her. Patsy said the best advice she was ever given about the Miss West Virginia reign was by the previous year's winner, Teresa Lucas, who told Patsy to enjoy every minute of every day of that year. And I think she did. Patsy was always able to enjoy the stage of her life she was in. She never seemed to long for the past or wish for the future. She had a good time being "Patricia Ann Paugh, Miss West Virginia" and she also had a good time being just plain old Patsy.

When her year as Miss West Virginia was over, Patsy continued her college education and I quit teaching the next year to have our first child. Patsy and her mom and sisters held a baby shower for me. She hand-painted a toy box for me that I still have in my foyer.

So we have another phase in a life where we can find no hidden secrets. There is no dark side here--no built-up hostility or examples of deviant behavior. There's nothing to look back on which might cause someone to later become a monster. She was a talented young lady with a loyal family and good friends. This is just another chapter in the life of someone who was good and kind and genuine and generous and happy. And she made others happy.

Patsy's family moved to Charleston, WV, at the end of 1977, when Pam had graduated from high school. We wouldn't see each other very often, but we stayed in touch and our paths crossed at several important times in our lives.

Patsy's college photo, 1979.

Patsy with local Cadillac-Olds dealer, Dan Wharton. Miss West Virginia's "official" car.

I quit teaching to have a baby. Patsy hand-painted a toy chest and held a baby shower for me. This is a photo of Patsy holding my son, Jim, and a family friend, Christopher, summer of 1979.

Chapter Four:
Sisters Pam and Paulette

I originally planned for this project to include only Patsy's friends. But when her sisters, Pam and Paulette (Polly) heard about it, they asked if they, too, could tell their stories. "She is more than just our sister," they said, "she is a best friend." I don't have a sister, but I know the bonds of sisterhood can be very strong. The three Paugh girls are no exception. Patsy's sisters both live in Atlanta and struggle each day with their dilemma--loving Patsy with all of their hearts and yet not being able to do anything to stop the vicious speculation about her. They shared their sister with us:

Pam is two and half years younger than Patsy:

"Patsy was always the one to do what she was told. I was the hard-headed child who questioned 'why'. Patsy was very predictable; I'm very unpredictable. Patsy loved to play arts and crafty things, draw pictures, make projects, dress up in costumes. I was the tomboy who liked to play cowboys and Indians and climb trees. Patsy is organized and I am spontaneous. We couldn't have been more opposite in some ways, but we shared a wonderful childhood. I always knew how lucky I was to have her as a big sister. With such different personalities, it's hard to understand why we are so close. But we are.

"Did we argue like most siblings? No. But it wasn't because I didn't try. It's just that it takes two to argue and Patsy wouldn't. From childhood, she has been one of those peacemakers who seem to have the ability to calm a storm. I can't remember hearing her yell; I have often envied her inner peace. She is more than just polite; she doesn't like to see anyone upset and

would rather give in than fight. I think I used that to my advantage when I was younger and got my way more often than I should have with her. On the other hand, her calm personality was better suited to getting along in our household than my stubbornness. I remember getting in trouble with Mom and Dad; Patsy never seemed to.

"Patsy was always ready and willing to help her sisters and her friends. As members of the neighborhood swim team, Polly and I were pretty good swimmers but that was not one of Patsy's talents. I guess you could say 'she sat on the bench'. But one day the team needed her and she gave it her best. We needed a 4th member for a relay event to get enough points to win the meet. The coach told her, 'I don't care how fast you go--just get "in" the water and somehow manage to get from one end of the pool to the other without touching the bottom.' So Patsy did her version of the back-side paddle and the other members of the team made up for Patsy's slow time in their laps. We won! And I remember that the whole team cheered--for Patsy--for her spirit.

"We took dance lessons together though I soon realized that Patsy had the dancing talent; it was not for me. But when my parents got an electric organ, I discovered that playing music and singing were what I loved. And I guess I am grateful to our parents who helped each of their girls develop the talent that she wanted; they didn't expect the 3 of us to all do the same types of activities. They didn't compare us or measure us against each other.

"We shared so much and I realize now how lucky we were as children. I remember family gospel sing-alongs with Mom playing the piano. I remember neighborhood carnivals where we put on talent shows and sold tickets to the parents. I remember that Dad built us a big white playhouse with lights, curtains, and furniture. It was the hangout for the neighborhood kids. I remember that we all had to do our Saturday chores before we got our 25 cents to go to the roller skating rink up the street. Yes, we had a terrific childhood and we remain so close as a family.

"Pageants were something that we enjoyed as a part of our teenage years. They were fun and I think we liked performing just as we had in our family gatherings and neighborhood and church camp talent shows. The first time Patsy ever entered a contest was when she was nominated as DeMolay sweetheart

40

during her sophomore year of high school. Mom bought her a new dress at the local department store and she represented the local chapter in the state contest. She didn't win first place but she really had a great time. The next year she entered the Wood County Fair pageant and that time she did win. Her upside-down tap dance stole the show.

"Later, my Grandma Janie saw an advertisement in the local paper for 'Miss Bicentennial Teenager' and she told me she thought I should enter. This contest considers community service, academics, activities, awards, photos and recommendations. I was thrilled--and more than a little surprised--when I won in West Virginia. When my grandma had an angina attack and my mom couldn't go with me to the National Finals, Patsy agreed to be my chaperone. Winning that national title is one of the most exciting things that happened in my life and I owe a lot to my big sister for believing in me.

"When I decided to enter the Miss West Virginia pageant 3 years after Patsy had won, it was kind of a last minute decision. It was only 5 or 6 weeks ahead of time. I called Patsy and asked, 'Now what do I do?' She gave me lots of advice and I worked hard. I had confidence in my speaking ability and I knew I could handle the talent part, but I never thought I was pretty enough. I also knew I had the stigma of being a former Miss West Virginia's sister. So I was very surprised when I won and no one was happier for me than Patsy. I got tired of people asking if I had entered because of Patsy. When one of the judges asked how it felt to constantly be compared to my sister, I answered, 'If you knew my sister, you would know why I consider it an honor to be compared to her!'

"I first met John Ramsey at the Charleston, WV, airport when he came to meet Patsy's family. After the visit, we all agreed how much we liked him. He was rather quiet but he had a sense of humor. He was intelligent but down to earth. He was easy to talk to and I felt like I'd known him all my life. The real clincher was the way he treated my sister Patsy--with obvious love and respect.

"Since then, I have found John to be a wonderful listener. He is non-judgemental; he is fair; he always looks for the positives in other people. I have stayed in their home to baby sit for the children. I have worked for John at his company. We have gone through the best of times and the worst of times and I

have witnessed what a truly remarkable man he is.

"John is a thoughtful and caring man. When Grandma Janie's sister was dying of cancer, she had a craving for watermelon. It was in the winter and therefore there were no watermelons in West Virginia. John was in Florida on a business trip and when the restaurant served him a wedge of watermelon with his lunch, he bought a whole one and had it cold-packed and shipped to Parkersburg for her.

"Patsy and John are special people and perfectly suited for each other. They share their home with others. They are both such giving and caring people. They both have strong faith and they are a testament to their faith by the lives they lead.

"When I found out that Patsy had cancer, I was in Denver. I flew all night to get to her. I am very religious but I found myself asking God, 'Why her? Why not me? She has the children to raise; she has lived such a good life.' My sister Patsy faced cancer like she faced everything else in life--with strength and with absolute faith that she could meet the challenge. She never complained. I have seen her so sick that she had to be carried. Her body was so wasted and fevered that she couldn't keep anything down. She couldn't even stand sunlight on her face. And through it all, she comforted us.

"With our family history, Patsy's doctor suggested that we were at high risk for ovarian cancer, too. I made the decision to have a hysterectomy. My nieces and nephews are the only children I will ever have. I love them as my own. I don't think I ever will be able to cope with the loss of JonBenét. And I hate most of all the pain that my sister has to suffer.

"I am angry. I am very angry. The death of JonBenét devastated us all. But the awful lies and accusations have hurt beyond description. To watch someone you love suffer is bad enough. . .but then to watch her falsely accused by people who do not know her. . .is almost too much to bear. I want to scream at the world to leave her alone!

"The word respect isn't good enough for Patsy. She is the daughter every mother wishes she had, the wife every man dreams of, the mother every child deserves. And she is the sister I have been blessed to call mine. I love her deeply and I believe in her absolutely."

signed: Pamela Ellen Paugh

Polly is seven years younger than Patsy:

"I was in elementary school when Patsy was in high school. You can imagine how much I looked up to an older sister who was not only pretty on the outside but also lovely on the inside. My earliest memories of Patsy are of her helping me or playing with me. She never treated me like a little pest that she didn't want around her friends. She never was too busy to answer my questions. She was always willing to let me join in the games. She was always willing to share.

"For some reason, I vividly remember Patsy, Pam and I playing our silly version of 'Let's Make a Deal.' We would hide something 'valuable' (like a stuffed animal or an old wallet) behind the closet doors and someone would choose between 'Door #1, Door #2 or Door #3'. I'm sure now that they were doing these things to entertain me, but we always had such a good time!

"We used to go on family camping / fishing trips. We would borrow Uncle Ken's trailer and take off for the state park. We had Boston Terriers and I remember one named Cinder. He used to snore so badly that we had to keep him in the bathroom of the camper. I loved those family trips. As I look back now, I realize how much we did together as a family. I thank my parents for that. It's probably one of the reasons we are all so close now.

"One thing we were taught from an early age was to help others. But our mom showed us how to help and have fun at the same time. She would load the 3 of us and our friends into the station wagon and we would go around to Senior Citizen Centers to entertain. Patsy would tap dance; Pam would sing; I had the 'animal act.' One of our dogs (Cinderella) could 'speak.' She could make noises that sounded just like the words 'momma' and 'I love you'. So they let me be a part of the show with my talking dog.

"We used to decorate bicycles to be in parades. It was another family affair. Dad was the engineer and Mom was the designer. We would get pretty elaborate with umbrellas, flowers, and patriotic music coming from the basket. Later, Patsy would do the same thing with her children. Once they decorated Burke's bike as a pirate ship with a treasure chest. JonBenét's had an Olympic theme, with five rings made out of colored foil. As I watched them parade their bikes, I smiled and remembered our own parades so many years ago. I vowed that I would try to be

43

as good a mother for my children as my mom and Patsy are!

"I was in the seventh grade when I sat in the audience and heard the announcer say, 'Miss West Virginia for 1977 is.... Patricia Ann Paugh'. It was quite a thrill for a little sister! Later Patsy would offer to let me wear her pageant dresses for my ninth and tenth grade proms (see photos). Mom offered to buy me a new dress, but I loved the idea of dressing up like my sister Patsy! Later, after Patsy and Pam had both been crowned Miss West Virginia, people would ask me if I felt any pressure to enter a pageant. No, I didn't. Not at all. My parents were great about encouraging each of us to do what we liked best. My love was music.

"I played the flute and was in the marching and concert bands. In my sophomore year I decided to try out for the drill team. Patsy came home from college to help me. She choreographed a dance routine for me to the song Copa Cabana. I had a fruit hat; I guess I was supposed to look like Carmen Miranda. I was nervous; I had never done anything like this before. But Patsy and Mom worked with me and I practiced and practiced. I made the team and I know I had my big sis to thank--as I would thank her for so much more in my life.

"I guess what I now realize is so surprising is that there was no competition among the sisters. Our family came first. We all knew we were loved and we all were appreciated for what we were. Mom and Dad taught us to try our hardest, do our best and have the self-confidence to know we could succeed. And they taught us to be gracious when we lost. These are lessons a parent should teach; these are the lessons I will pass along to my children.

"I spent summers of my high school years working at John's business in Atlanta. They opened their house to me and I could talk to Patsy about anything. I loved being with her. After college, I moved to Atlanta and went to work full-time for John's company.

"A year later Burke was born. I was thrilled. We were all at the hospital and when John came into the waiting room with a big smile on his face and announced, "It's a boy," I cried. John had picked the name Burke because he liked it; Patsy had picked the middle name Hamilton--after the middle name of a childhood friend. Pam and I loved to babysit. I don't think Patsy ever had to leave Burke with a strange sitter; Aunt Polly and Aunt

Pam tried our best to spoil him, but he's turned out to be a terrific kid!

"When JonBenét arrived 3 1/2 years later, she came so fast that she was almost born in the car. When I got to the hospital, I met John at the emergency room admissions desk. I was excited and I thought he said Patsy was on the fourth floor. I took the elevator and looked all over the fourth floor. When I finally got back downstairs, I found out he said the fourth room, not the fourth floor. I noticed he had worn a pink knit golf shirt and pink shorts in honor of his newest girl.

"In 1993 I was pregnant with my first child when I found out that my sister Patsy had ovarian cancer. I was in shock. Not Patsy! After her surgery and first chemotherapy treatment, we were not allowed in her room. I stood at the door, pregnant and distraught and she comforted me, saying, 'Don't worry, Polly, everything will be okay. Have faith in God.' But it was so hard to take. I cried as I watched her walk slowly to the window to watch her children play outside.

"I don't know if that had anything to do with my going into labor 6 weeks early, but I know that it was the most stressful time in our lives. But even in her misery, she sent me flowers and called me at the hospital. Thinking of others has always been a natural part of Patsy's life.

"Patsy is as good a sister as anyone could ever hope to have. She is a wonderful mother and aunt. She is a best friend. She is our strength. She is always there for me and I will always be there for her. I love her with all my heart!"

signed: Paulette Paugh Davis

These two people have literally known Patsy all of their lives. They are more than just a chapter in her life; they are entwined throughout it. I wish I could adequately describe the intense, overwhelming love and devotion that I felt as I talked with them about their sister Patsy. And the pain. . .the frustration. . .the anger. . .the helplessness that they suffer because they cannot do more to help the sister who has done so much for them. It's a tragedy that has grown, not diminished, as time goes on.

Patsy, Paulette and Pam Paugh.

Pam and Paulette were two of Patsy's bridesmaids.

For Christmas 1985, the girls and John had this photo taken to give to their parents.

Patsy congratulates sister Pam when Pam was chosen Miss South
Charleston and would be an entrant in the Miss West Virginia finals.

Later, Pam changed for this "informal" family photo. Notice Don with his usual sense of humor.

Patsy on the runway in Atlantic City during the Miss America Pageant.

Paulette wore sister Patsy's pageant gown to her ninth-grade prom.

Linda McLean and Pam board the governor's jet to ride to the Miss America Pageant in Atlantic City. Pam was Miss West Virginia, 1980.

The Paughs have had several Boston Terriers. One, named Cinderella, could say "mama."

Chapter Five:
Move to Atlanta
and Marriage to John

I met several of Patsy's friends in Atlanta. Some of them have known her for close to twenty years; one just met her last year, months after the tragedy. But they, like everyone I have talked to, share unwavering faith in Patsy's goodness. They, too, want to let the world know the truth about this wonderful woman. I will just let them tell you their own stories.

Claudia:

"Twenty years ago, when my husband's younger sister Stephanie and her college friend Patsy came to visit us just after they graduated from college, they drove 2 cars. That was because his sister was going to stay and Patsy was probably going to go back to West Virginia. But Patsy decided to stay in Atlanta, too. The girls lived with us in our one-bedroom apartment while they looked for a place of their own.

"We didn't have much money to go out, so we often went to the apartment complex pool. That's where my husband and I had met John Ramsey about two weeks before the girls came to town. John was divorced and lived in the apartment upstairs. My husband and John talked about computers. We had started a graphic software business and John was a distributor of microcomputers. We had a common bond and thought we could meet each other's business needs. We also just liked him. And we had invited John to dinner.

"Patsy and Stephanie had been out sightseeing all day and returned in their casual clothes, energetic and full of excitement about being in the 'big city.' My husband told them that Mr. Ramsey was coming to dinner to discuss business so they'd

better calm down and act mature! They did and we had a great dinner.

"Since the lack of money had forced us to find 'home entertainment,' we were used to playing card games or 'spoons'. That night we decided to play charades. During the fun, John suddenly looked at his watch and said, 'I have to leave for a while.' We thought maybe we were being too silly for him. But he did return later. We often got together after that and each night about 8:00 he would leave; we didn't ask him why. Later we would find out that he called his children every night--wherever he was, whatever he was doing. And he did that for all the years they were growing up.

"I was out of town when my husband told me on the phone that John had asked Patsy for a date. It was not something we had expected, so this was a pleasant surprise since we liked them both so much. When Patsy and Stephanie moved to their own apartment, John and Patsy began dating more often, but not exclusively. Patsy had recently broken up with a long-time college boyfriend and she wasn't ready for a full-time relationship. I don't think John was, either.

"That fall, we moved out of the apartment complex at the same time John did. My husband and I had scraped together enough money for a down payment on a starter house. John had bought a small 'fixer-upper'. We shared a Ryder rental truck to save money. It was pouring rain. Because we had to be out of our apartment at the end of the month, we found ourselves moving out on Friday but not closing on the houses until Monday. So we had to spend the weekend in a cheap motel and had to climb into the rental truck to get clean clothes. I smile as I look back on those younger days; we were carefree and nothing fazed us.

"John liked to fly. He was in the navy reserves and therefore could rent airplanes at a reduced rate. Patsy was afraid to fly at first, but later learned to enjoy it. As they grew closer, they found many things they shared in common. They seemed so right for each other. John took Patsy back to our old apartment complex and proposed to her at the side of the pool. They were married in November 1980, about a year and a half after they had met.

"When I became pregnant, Patsy was as excited as we were. She wanted to know everything! She wanted to put her hand on my stomach to feel the kicks. She asked lots of questions

54

and seemed amazed at the process. At our first dinner together after we found out that we were pregnant, Patsy put mustard into my husband's napkin. When he opened the messy napkin, she said it was so he could get used to 'dirty diapers.' Both Patsy and John have a wonderful sense of humor.

"When I was getting things ready for the baby, I asked Patsy if she would paint something on the wall of the nursery. I had in mind a big sun or a teddy bear. But I should have known Patsy. She designed and sketched a mural that included Cinderella, Raggedy Ann and Andy, Winnie-the-Pooh, Alice in Wonderland and more. (see photo). She spent days painting it on our wall. We were amazed and touched. When we left that house, I hated to part with the mural. The last time I checked, it was still on the wall; the new owners said they liked it, too. This is an example of how Patsy always goes above and beyond. She gives every commitment, every project, every task 110% of herself. She's an incredible friend to have.

"Our lives have gone through transitions with the demands of children and geographic moves, but Patsy and John have remained very close friends. We may go months without seeing each other and yet when we get together, it's like we just saw them yesterday.

"When I first heard about the death of JonBenét, I was really afraid for them. They had lost their oldest daughter, then John's father, then Patsy had struggled with cancer. Now they had lost their youngest child. I didn't know how much any human beings could take.

"I realize that parents are sometimes suspected in cases like this, but I couldn't believe it when some of the media began to take it seriously. The possibility that it would go this far was beyond me. I had faith that the police would soon discover how good these two people are and they would get on with finding the real murderer. But they didn't.

"That's why I want to finally speak out. People need to know the truth. For too many months, people have heard only one side. It is so frustrating. The truth doesn't sell newspapers. So I just have to say that I would give all I own for the world to know that these wonderful, unselfish people could not have been involved in any way. They are good people. They are good friends."
signed: Claudia McCutcheon

Marcia:

"I first met Patsy and John at church in the early 1980s; they were one of the six original couples who started 'Couples in Christ,' our Sunday school class. We were in this class with the Ramseys for 6 or 7 years. Most of us started out in the class as newlyweds with no children. We were quite a mixed group, with different backgrounds and different careers but we grew together as we had our children and strengthened our faith.

"Each Sunday we had lessons on marriage, child-raising, and social issues. We discussed how the topic related to the Bible and to God. It was a warm, interesting, vibrant group and we also socialized outside of the church. We had children's holiday parties (like an Easter Egg Hunt). We took weekend trips together with our families. At Thanksgiving, we would have a special dinner and each person would share what he or she was thankful for. It was an emotional, bonding experience and we have remained close since that time.

"Some of the men from the class formed a 'lunch bunch' and they have been together ever since, even though they have all gone in separate directions and belong to other churches. About 2 years ago, several close women friends who had originally met in the Sunday School class started our own group called 'Eleven is Heaven.' We meet once a month to continue our friendship and to share our lives over lunch. Since she moved back to Atlanta, Patsy has become part of this group. Despite everything that has happened, she always tries to have a good time and make those around her feel relaxed.

"You just feel better when you are with her. She is always aware of what is going on in others' lives. She is always ready to share the load. 'Sincerity' is a word that describes her well. She is also full of creative ideas. Volunteer work is a big part of Patsy's character and she does it so naturally and so well. She is the same wonderful person we met over fifteen years ago and we would do anything to ease her pain.

"We knew John and Patsy before they became wealthy. She was just as giving then of her talents, her money and her time. She always comes up with something extra special that makes every event even more memorable. She always goes above and beyond to make others happy. In February, 6 of us 'girls' spent the weekend at a friend's home in another state. It was just prior to Valentine's Day. Patsy showed up with glitter and glue and paper and scissors and paints. We had so much fun making homemade valentines for our families. We know this was hard for her because she had always told us how much JonBenét enjoyed this particular holiday.

"It's like that with her family, friends and her work for charity. Patsy has a gift of giving. She encourages others to give just by her example. It's like a magical effect. And she never wants the credit. She is selfless, making an effort to include everyone and wanting to give others the credit. I have worked with Patsy on fund-raising projects. She is able to organize and inspire others to do their best. She plans everything to the last detail and then makes it seem more like fun than work. She may not be a saint, but she sure is as close to one as I have seen.

"My mother died when I was fifteen. My father remarried; there were 4 children in my family and 3 in my stepmother's. But it wasn't like the Brady Bunch. It was hard to combine into one group--to form a blended family. So I was really amazed at the love in the Ramsey household, with the three children from John's first marriage and two of John and Patsy's together. There were never two families, always just one. There was no jealousy or animosity. They were always 'our' children, never the 'stepchildren.' Patsy had a special relationship with Beth, Melinda and John Andrew; after all, they were only eleven, eight and four when John and Patsy married (see color photo 2). And they remained amiable with John's first wife, Cindy, and her new husband. Cindy was always at family special events. This mature relationship was good for everyone, especially the children.

"When we got a phone call from a friend telling us about JonBenét, I couldn't breathe. My heart stopped. I really think I was in a state of shock. For some reason I suddenly remembered a day when Patsy was sick and I took my daughter and JonBenét (both 3 years old) to see Snow White. Although it was a children's movie, there were parts in it, like the wicked witch, which scared the girls a little. So they both sat in my lap. I could feel the presence of JonBenét that same night in my home, on my lap. I could hear her laughter and feel her energy. It was so unbelievable that she was gone from our world.

"In addition to the grief, I worried about Patsy's health. How could anyone find the strength to face this? Patsy loved her children so much! When they flew into Atlanta from Boulder for the funeral, we were among a group of friends who met them at

*the airport. Patsy looked at me and said, 'Hold your children
every day and tell them that you love them.' And I have.*

*"There isn't a day that goes by that I don't thank God for
my children. I realize how precious they are. I hold my daughter
more, I hug her more, I tell her I love her more. . .and I am more
patient. JonBenét's death was tragic but even from this tragedy
comes gifts to others--strength and love and encouragement to
be better parents and to realize what really is important.*

*"One of the things Patsy and I share is our complete faith
in God. Knowing Patsy and all that she has been through and
then hearing her witness and recite scripture and knowing that
she still clings to God has strengthened all of us. She doesn't just
talk her faith, she walks it and lives it and shares it every day.*

*"I pray every day for God to give Patsy and John the
faith and strength to start their day. I believe that our God has
to be proud of Patsy. She has been His faithful servant. She is an
example of the best we can be. By knowing her I am a better
person. She genuinely loves God, loves her family and loves her
friends. And we genuinely love her."*

signed: Marcia Shurley

Mary :

*"My husband and I met John and Patsy through mu-
tual friends and we have been friends for 18 years. Patsy and I
were pregnant for our first child at the same time; their son Burke
is about 2 weeks older than our son. We shared the day-to-day
excitement of young mothers-to-be. We talked about everything
from names to nausea. We wondered how we would react in labor and we wondered how we would raise our children. We were
determined to be the best parents ever!*

*"Patsy and John and my husband and I were members
of the same church and a group of us 'girls' from the church
started to go to lunch once a month. With tongue in cheek, we
called ourselves the 'Socie-tea' bunch. It was a play on words
because we were anything but formal. Patsy, ever the organizer,
printed a newsletter and made the plans. The group ended up
growing to 20 or 30. It finally got too complicated and when
Patsy moved, the group just faded away. She was the glue that
held us together.*

*"I was chairman of an organization called TWIGS, a
neighborhood fundraising group for a local children's hospital.*

My friend Patsy pitched right in and helped us with a major project for the fund--creating Christmas cards from children's art work. That year the project raised 3 times as much as it ever had. I knew much of this could be credited to Patsy's dedication and energy.

"One thing I remember most is Patsy's love for the Christmas season. We went to their annual Christmas party. As with everything she did, it was extraordinary. Santa was there with gifts for the children. They had a player piano and we would all sing Christmas carols. We shared other great times together from children's birthday parties to our couples dinner group. It was a wonderful time in our lives. We were living the American dream, with friends and family. Life was good.

"Then, in the Spring of 1990, I was diagnosed with breast cancer. After my initial surgery, it was Patsy who scheduled friends to bring meals to my home, helped with the shopping, brought me little special treats, and was always there with a smile to help my family with anything and everything I needed. I will never forget how much she did for me. I will forever be grateful for her support.

"So when I heard that Patsy had been diagnosed with ovarian cancer, I wanted to be there for her. Even though she was in Boulder for much of the time and I was in Atlanta, I prayed for her every day. I wished there was more I could do. Having both fought cancer, I feel we have a special bond. No matter how long we are apart, all we have to do is pick up the phone and we are right there for each other again.

"About an hour after I opened the Ramsey's 1996 Christmas card, my husband told me the devastating news about JonBenét. I still can't believe it. But more than that, I can't believe that anyone could think that Patsy could have been involved in any way.

"Patsy has blessed my life and the lives of all those she has touched. Her honesty, her integrity, her genuine goodness and her strong faith shine through every aspect of her life. I am fortunate to know her. I believe in her with all my heart and soul."

signed: Mary Justice

Regina:

"*In August of 1997 I had just moved to Atlanta from New York. My husband had been transferred here and I was upset abut leaving my family and friends. I guess you could say I came 'kicking and screaming.' We moved on the 23rd and our son started school on the 25th. So when I showed up at the first 'Fifth grade parents meeting,' I didn't know anyone. And, being from New York, I was certainly dressed more casually than most of the other moms. (Would you believe I wore jeans?) I remember standing by myself and thinking how much I didn't want to be there.*

"*Then Patsy introduced herself to me. She was so nice and seemed so friendly and outgoing. We started talking about our sons and about our recent moves to the area. She invited me to have a cup of coffee and during that first hour together I knew I really liked her.*

"*There was a night meeting at the school a few days later and my husband was out of town. So Patsy invited me to drop my son off at her house to play with Burke; her sister was babysitting. By the end of the night, my son was calling Patsy's sister 'Aunt Pam.' He had found a second home. Our sons have become best friends. Burke is quieter; Josh is more energetic. But they seemed to click and I think they complement each other. They both like the normal kids activities--Nintendo, computer games, Little League. I am pleased that they are friends because Burke is such a great kid--easy going and nice to be around.*

"*At the second school meeting, Patsy took great care to introduce me to other parents that she knew. It was the first time I realized what I would later come to find is so much a part of her. She always thinks of others; she is always willing to give of herself. With all that she's been through, she is still willing to open up and trust other people. She still believes that people, in general, are good.*

"*We get together almost every morning for coffee and conversation. We sometimes exercise together. We have dinner together with our husbands and sons most every Friday night. Our sons sleep overnight at each other's house all the time. She trusts her child with me; I trust my child with her. She is such a good mom. She never raises her voice (like I do). She is patient and kind and fun to be around. The time I have spent with Patsy hasn't been quantity, but it has been quality. I could tell her any-*

thing--and I have. I feel very close to her and am proud to call her my friend.

"She is one of the least pretentious people I have ever met; she's so real. There's no phoniness or arrogance about her. Once I saw the kind of person she really is, I thought, 'If only people knew this person I have come to know, they would realize that she couldn't be involved with anything like what the media implies.' I have had friends in New York, who upon learning I am friends with Patsy, have asked me, 'Are you sure about her?' Yes, I am absolutely sure about her!!

"I have seen her at her best and I have seen her at her worst. I've shared her tears about JonBenét. Yet there are times when we share laughter, too. She has a great sorrow and yet a tremendous capacity for joy. The night she came to the school talent show to see our son playing the piano, she got upset and had to leave when a little blonde girl played the violin. I realized that she lives with the pain just under the surface all of the time.

"Sometimes when couples go through tragedy, it tears them apart. But I can see the bond between John and Patsy is still strong. There is a lot of warmth between them. They are there for each other to lean on. They put things in perspective and realize what is important and what is not. It is so unfair for anyone to think that either of these people could be involved.

"Patsy is an unselfish, beautiful soul. You meet so few people like this in your life. I feel blessed to know her."

signed: Regina Orlick

I was touched by the stories that these Atlanta friends told, by the tears in their eyes during parts of their conversations. Every one of them used the words, "I am blessed to know Patsy." They, like the rest of us, were all devastated by the loss of a child, but also now by the brutal attacks on their friend. They want the world to know the wonderful person they have known. And so they are willing to sign their names and share their memories in hopes that, in some small way, they can help.

And this is another chapter in the life of this special person, another chapter which has no stories of jealousy or arrogance or foul moods or strange behavior. It is consistent with the rest of her life. Patsy has a heart that cares and a soul that shares. She enriches the lives of everyone she touches.

I first met John in 1980 when Pam won the Miss South Charleston contest. He kept his beard for their wedding that November.

For years, John and Patsy joined friends to vacation in Highlands, NC. They missed only the year that Patsy was taking chemotherapy.

When Patsy's friend asked her to paint a picture on the wall of her nursery, Patsy did this elaborate nursery rhyme mural, 1981.

Chapter Six:
Patsy, the Mother

Patsy is a wonderful mother. This is one of the consistent things I have heard from everyone I spoke to. She became a loving "special mom" to Beth, Melinda and John Andrew when she and John were married. They were young when Patsy first met them and she enjoyed not only playing with them and teaching them, but also learning from them about this new role of parent.

Burke Hamilton Ramsey was born January 27, 1987, and JonBenét Patricia Ramsey was born on August 6, 1990. Patsy's life seemed to be everything that she could ask for and all that she had dreamed. But the dream became a nightmare.

Melinda and John Andrew miss their older sister, Beth who died in a 1992 automobile accident and their younger sister, JonBenét. It hurts them to watch their father and Patsy suffer. It was painful, but they were willing to share their memories and their feelings. If anyone would know about Patsy as a mother, it would be her children (*see color photo 6*).

From Melinda:

"I've never called her mother, because I already have a wonderful mother; I call her Patsy. But I think of her as my 'special mom'. I first met Patsy when I was seven or eight years old, after my parents had been divorced for a couple of years. For some reason, one of my first impressions was that she seemed so full of energy. As we got to know each other, we became very close and we still are. We are not related by blood, but we are related by love.

"Patsy was always so much fun to be around! I vividly remember the family playing Bingo and Charades together. When

it was our birthday, she always made a fuss. This was our 'special day' and the birthday child was the center of attention. Patsy was always interested in whatever I was doing in school. I remember when I ran for the student council in junior high, she helped me make posters and buttons and practice my speech. Patsy always thinks of others. She always puts other people's feelings, wants and needs above her own. It makes her happy to make other people happy. And that's what makes her so special.

"I know it's hard to be a step-parent. You are somewhere in the middle--like a "fill in". But Patsy was always genuinely glad to see us; she treated us like her own children. It meant a lot to me as a child when she introduced me to people as "My daughter, Melinda". She didn't make the distinction of "step child." But she also didn't cross the line and try to become our mother. She didn't discipline us. For my upcoming wedding, she and my mother are working together as a team. Patsy helped Mom select the invitations and organize my engagement party. I know I am fortunate to have a family like this.

"One day as we were driving in the car, Dad asked, 'What would you think about having another brother or sister?' It really caught me off-guard and I was shocked; I guess I just never thought about it. But I was really happy and when Burke and JonBenét were born, it was so exciting! They were both so much fun to be around. Burke liked to play with John Andrew, always looking for him to play matchbox cars, etc. JonBenét and I liked to paint together or play dress up. Each year we colored Easter Eggs and we had a Christmas tradition of baking cookies together.

"Since I grew up in Georgia, I wasn't used to snow. One day in Boulder, there were little patches of snow on the ground and JonBenét and I went out to 'build a snowman'. I soon realized that it would be almost impossible to do this with the little bit of snow that was left. But JonBenét was determined. 'I know we can do it!' And so, of course, we worked and worked until we had a two-foot high snowman. I'd do anything to make her happy.

"One of my strongest memories is how she always ran to greet me. Her pigtails were flying, her hands were outstretched and she screamed, 'Be-winda, Be-winda'. It is this memory that I cherish the most.

"It breaks my heart to see these horrible accusations being made about Dad and Patsy. They are wonderful parents!

1. Judy Mason Schoch, Diane Dunn McClure, Debbie Shepler Krieg and Patsy with husbands at high school reunion party. Debbie and Patsy are first cousins and have always looked remarkably alike.

2. John and Patsy were married in November, 1980. Patsy made the flower girl dresses for Melinda and Beth; Grandma helped with the little tuxedo for John Andrew.

3. Patsy struggled with Stage IV ovarian cancer and won. She desperately wanted to live to raise her children. Her faith in God, the love of her family and friends, and strong, experimental medical treatment helped her conquer the disease.

4. John and Patsy took all five children hiking. Here JonBenét sleeps peacefully in dad's backpack.

5. Burke, Patsy and JonBenét on the first day of school. Burke (9) was in fourth grade; JonBenét (6) was in kindergarten.

6. Boating on the lake in Michigan. Melinda, Patsy, JonBenét, John Andrew, John and Burke.

7. This picture of author, Linda McLean and her husband Jim was taken at an office Christmas party. Just months later, Jim was diagnosed with Stage IV stomach cancer. He died in 1995.

8. In October, 1997, Patsy and her mother came back to Parkersburg, WV to visit family and friends. They attended Sunday morning service at Patsy's childhood church, Stout Memorial.

Patsy helped raise Beth and John Andrew and me. I watched them with Burke and JonBenét. I know! And yet people who don't know them, who have never even met them, are saying absolutely horrible things! They have no right to!!

"I'm their daughter. I've lived under the same roof with them. I had the same parents as JonBenét. I have such a hard time understanding why the public refuses to believe me--why my word just isn't enough.

"I'm glad Dad and Patsy are strong people. They have withstood a lot and they can withstand this, too. But it isn't fair. It just isn't fair!"

Melinda Bennett Ramsey, age 26

At this point, Melinda was crying and I told her that we didn't have to continue. But it was so obvious to me that she loved Patsy completely and that she was suffering, yet another victim of this tragedy. Then I spoke to her brother.

From John Andrew:

"I was very young when Dad met Patsy and I don't remember much about the first years. I know I was comfortable in both homes and, although I knew Patsy wasn't my mom, she had that role when I was with her and my dad. She encouraged us in our activities but never pushed us into anything. She was interested in all that I did, whether it was Boy Scouts, sports or school activities. I have good memories of growing up. It's not just the vacations and special times, but it's the general everyday things that made a loving and caring family relationship.

"I am 10 years older than Burke but we can still enjoy Play Station together! I was 14 years older than JonBenét and I loved her very much. . .we made lemonade together. I know it is accurate to call them 'half' brother and sister, but none of us has ever felt we have half a relationship. Burke and JonBenét are my brother and my sister. They've never called me 'half' brother; they call me 'big' brother.

"And I resent having to even talk about Dad and Patsy like this. I don't see a need to defend our family. Why do we keep having to say that we are a normal family? The outlandish, false things that are said are just what the media has made up about us. There is nothing previously in our lives to indicate that we

71

are anything but a loving family and yet we have to keep defend-
ing ourselves. Dad and Patsy are great parents. What else can I
say?"

John Andrew Ramsey, age 22

John Andrew was angry and I can't say I blame him. Like Melinda's tears, his anger was just one more painful result of this public spectacle. What an awful thing for these young people to have to face. And yet they are strong like the elder Ramseys and I know they will get through this.

Lanie Lopez babysat for Burke and JonBenét for years. She wanted to put her feelings into this book and said that the easiest way for her to write her feelings toward Patsy was as if she were writing her a letter.

Here are the unedited words of a 15-year-old girl written to Patsy:

Dear Patsy,

I don't know if I'll ever be able to express to you just how much you and your family mean to me, but I sure am going to try now. Tonight as I sat here writing this letter I thought back to the very first night I met you. I remember how welcome you made me feel in your home the very first time I baby-sat for Burke and JonBenét. You were probably one of the most friendly and outgoing people I had ever met. I remember going home that night and telling my mom how I hoped you would call me to baby-sit again soon, because you were the nicest lady I had ever met, and Burke and JonniB were the sweetest most well behaved kids I'd ever watched before.

Not only did you call me to baby-sit again, but also you welcomed me in as if I was part of your family. One of my many favorite things to do with you guys was to take part in your infamous bonfires. I so enjoyed watching you and the kids sing karioke around the bonfire while roasting hot-dogs and s'mores. Even though I have a terrible singing voice, I always felt comfortable enough around you guys to sing right along with you.

I want you to know that to me you're not just a mother of two of the kids I've baby-sat for, but you are like a second mom to me. I care about you as if you were a part of my family, not just a friend. I know that you're someone I can always talk to, and you'll always be there for me. That is the Patsy Ramsey that the rest of the world needs to see not the Patsy Ramsey that the news media makes you out to be.

This may not mean a lot to some people, because after all I'm just a fifteen year old kid, but I just want everyone and especially you Patsy, to know that from the very minute I found out about what had happened to JonBenét, the thought never even crossed my mind that you or John had anything to do with this awful tragedy. I know that you are the best mother (next to my own) that any child in this whole world could be blessed with. JonBenét was a very lucky little girl to have had you as a mother while she was here with us on earth, and I know that JonBenét is living a wonderful life with God in heaven. You and John love your children more than anyone could ever imagine, and I personally think that anyone that ever even thought you guys had something to do with JonBenét's death is crazy.

I know I have told you before just how much Burke and JonniB mean to me, but I just wanted to tell you again. Not a day goes by that I don't think about JonBenét and how much I miss her. I loved her like she was my little sister, and never will I forget all the fun times we shared together. I want to thank you for giving me the opportunity to spend as much time with JonBenét as I did, her incredible personality, sparkling eyes, and beautiful blonde hair changed my life forever.

In closing I want you to know what an awesome impact you have had on my life as a young adult. From you I've learned how to move past people's appearances and get to know their true qualities and also I've learned that no matter how tough life gets, with the help of friends and family there is always tomorrow. I also want to tell you again that no matter what happens in our lives, I will always be there for you and I'll always believe in you. Like I say, I love you as if you were my second mom. After JonBenét died you told me that you expected me to remain as close to you guys as before, and that you expected to be at my graduation and my wedding. Well, I hope to always remain close to you, John, and Burke, for the rest of my life. And yes, I, too expect you to be there when I graduate high school, college, and also be there with me when I get married. I want you to stay part of my life forever.

I hope you now know just how deeply I care for you, and that I always will. And I hope that all of you out there that don't know Patsy for who she is, you just know her for what the media

has portrayed her to be, realized after reading this that she is
one of the most incredible women in this world.

My love always,
Lanie Lopez

They say "a picture is worth 1000 words." The pictures at the end of this chapter of Burke and JonBenét as they grew show the obvious pride and joy their parents felt for them (*see also color photos 4 and 5*). We can see well-loved and nurtured children that were part of a big, wonderful extended family.

These are children who were wanted and loved and spoiled a little and fairly disciplined. They laughed and played like all children. Their parents dressed them with pride for the holiday pictures and they wore sweat suits and oversized T-shirts for play. Look carefully at these pictures. These are your children. These are my children. And their parents obviously loved and cared for them. They would never hurt them. We who know these parents understand this with every ounce of our being.

Burke's eighth birthday. They had a Laser Storm and pizza party.
Patsy makes each birthday special.

Lanie was JonBenét's babysitter and friend. Here they are on the Mackinac Island ferry in July 1995.

Ice skating in New York, November 1996.

Thanksgiving in Atlanta with Melinda (23), John, John Andrew (18), Burke (7) and JonBenét (4).

Burke's First Christmas 1987, 11 months old.

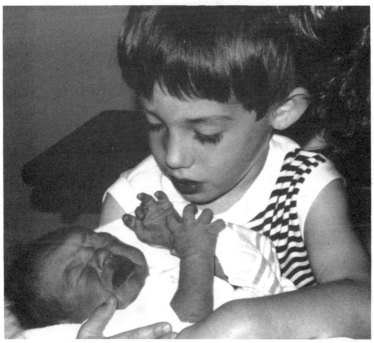

It seems like all families have a photo of the newborn crying on the older child's lap. Here, Burke holds JonBenét.

Easter 1994 in Ramsey's Boulder backyard. Each year they had an Easter Egg/Treasure Hunt for the children.

JonBenét wasn't the only one who got to dress up. This is Burke in the Ramsey living room in Atlanta, probably a year old.

Boulder Christmas parade. Despite her struggle with cancer, Patsy designed this float for the Cub Scout troop. She provided the red noses and music for them to sing along. Grandpa Don helped build the float and JonBenét wanted to ride, too.

"4-H Fair," Summer 1996 "My Collection".

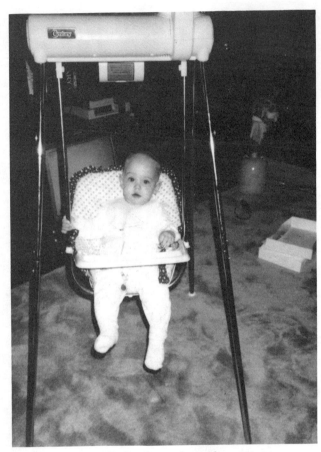

JonBenét goes for a ride.

JonBenét and Burke swimming at the old neighborhood pool during reunion trip--with daughter of Patsy's high school friend, Diane.

Patsy takes JonBenét for a visit to daddy's office.

Burke in Ramsey's Atlanta home.

JonBenét's first birthday party, August 1991.

I enjoyed getting Christmas photos from Patsy every year.

Although she fought and beat the cancer, Patsy wanted to be sure the kids saw Disney World just in case something happened to Mom. They took the trip in March 1995.

JonBenét and Patsy had so much fun together.

Chapter Seven:

Loss of Beth and the Struggle with Cancer

Patsy and John had it all: children, friends, career, home, religious faith and each other. Then, just when they least expected it, their world was turned upside down.

Sister Pam tells of the first of the tragedies:

"It was a cold drizzly January day in 1992 when we gathered at the cemetery. We were there to bury Beth, who was the eldest daughter of John and Cindy (his first wife). We all loved her so much and could not understand how this could happen. It seemed so wrong to lose her. How unfair, how senseless was this accident. Beth had graduated from Miami of Ohio the previous spring. While there, she had become active in a sorority and her passion was philanthropic work for the Cystic Fibrosis foundation. A young man whom she had grown very fond of (as a friend) was striken with the disease and it was her way of helping him fight it. Though the disease won, Beth remained active in research fundraising.

"Before graduation, her sorority held a senior banquet and I remember a poem John wrote for and recited to her:

"It talked about all of the 'firsts' they had experienced together. . .first word, first steps, first school days, first boyfriend, first prom, and now the first big steps she would boldly take into womanhood. Oh, how proud he was, and is, of her. Her smile and twinkling eyes were infectious. She had graduated with honors and there was every indication that she would succeed in her chosen field of finance. But before settling down to a 'desk

job' Beth decided that she would like to become a flight attendant and put to good use her fluent French and love for travel. She proudly wore her Delta Air Lines wings. She spoke often that Europe was her favorite place, although she also cherished quiet evenings in her new apartment.

"Beth was so excited when her new boyfriend asked her to visit his family in Chicago. It was mid-morning on January 8, as they were driving to the art museum to take in a special showing. The car tire hit a patch of ice on the entrance ramp to the highway, causing it to swerve across and into several lanes of fast-moving traffic. They were hit broadside by a truck. He was killed instantly; she was airlifted but pronounced DOA.

"I remember Dr. Frank Harrington telling a story during the funeral. It seemed to offer me some comfort at the time. It told of a young girl who walked daily with God. She would seek His advice, share her innermost thoughts, and strive to live according to His will. God was very pleased with her and one day as they walked and talked together, He pointed out that a day had not gone by when He wasn't at home in her house. 'But today,' God said, 'let's take a rest and go to my house.' And so she went. None of this story would have made much sense if it had not been for our strong Christian upbringing. JonBenét knew, even then, at age 2 1/2 that her sister Beth was now an angel and had gone to live with Jesus in Heaven. John and Cindy had asked me to sing at Beth's funeral service, a task I thought I was incapable of. But it was Patsy who took me aside and assured me that it was God Himself who would give me the calmness that was needed in such a situation. She told me to look at her and let God comfort the people through my voice. Later that day, Cindy and I shared a very special moment. I think it was at that time in our lives when she realized just how much our family loves her children.

"Later that year, it seemed everyone was going to Colorado skiing for Christmas Break. Well, almost everyone. When Patsy found out that Cindy was going to be all alone during the holidays, she would not have it. Patsy arranged for ALL of us to be together and I remember seeing the two of them standing in the dining room gazing out the window at the freshly fallen snow. Cindy was crying and Patsy was offering comfort. I heard her say to Cindy, 'We will get through this together.' And my eyes filled to see such compassion.

"In the months that followed, John and Patsy had a memorial chapel built to honor Beth's eternal life. It is located on the bottom floor of their Boulder church, St. John's Episcopal, and is dedicated to the Christian instruction of the children. What makes it such a special place is that everything is child-sized--the chairs, the altar, the maps in the study room, the BIBLE and even the Cross. JonBenét loved to be in the 'atrium' as it is called. There are structured classes where the children learn the teachings of Christ as well as how to live according to His promises. JonBenét used to tell everyone how she had a sister who is an angel. She loved being at church, period. She seemed to be re-energized there and Patsy and John took great care to be involved not only in adult worship and study, but to volunteer with planning 'lesson-oriented' children's activities. Though it was obvious that Patsy and John had the atrium built in Beth's memory, there are numerous other areas where their goodness and seed-planting have gone unannounced. These are the hearts of true and cheerful givers, the kind of giver Christ Himself spoke of. . .so it is no wonder that God has filled their lives with many blessings. Now that they are in Atlanta, I can be with them on a regular basis. It strengthens me to know that their faith in God, their love of family and their commitment to each other has not wavered."

signed: Pam

And just when they thought they had had enough anguish, more was to follow. In the summer of 1993, Patsy stopped by my office to see me on her way to serve as a judge for that year's Miss West Virginia pageant. My co-workers commented on how very pretty she is. There's something about her face that makes you smile; it generates warmth.

I enjoyed talking with her and we shared stories about our families. The next day, at the pageant, she noticed her jeans were really tight and she thought she was bloated. A week later, when she was in Michigan, she couldn't get her jeans fastened at all. Shortly after that, her sister called to tell me that Patsy had been diagnosed with an advanced stage of ovarian cancer. They moved fast; Patsy had surgery in Atlanta within two days.

Cousin Debbie remembers that time:

"After Patsy was diagnosed with cancer, I realized how fast time goes and how fragile life can be. We have become even closer because we now take the time to see each other more often. After the initial cancer surgery in July of 1993, I went to Atlanta to help take care of Burke and JonBenét. John had received a letter from the National Institutes of Health about the proposed chemotherapy and the possible horrible side effects. He was confused and upset, but determined to do whatever it took to help her. Since I am a nurse, he asked my opinion. I was honest with him, 'Since it's already in the lymph nodes, I don't think you have any choice.'

"John made the arrangements to enroll Patsy in the NIH program and was there for her as she battled for her life. Patsy and John had a solid relationship. Neither was overbearing; both were extremely considerate. They always supported each other and this time John became the steady rock that Patsy needed to lean on to help her through the crisis."

signed: Debbie

John flew with her to the National Institutes of Health in Bethesda, MD, and when she returned to Boulder, she was hospitalized with low blood counts. She spent months with her mother at her side to help. I remember her fierce determination to heal so that she could raise her children. She never spoke of wanting to live for herself; it was always, *"Please, God, let me survive so I can raise my children."*

Her faith was so strong. We spoke during her ordeal, but not often. Mostly I would call her mom to check on her. I sent her some books and cards and a stuffed bear I called AMY, full of hope and love. Patsy fought her battle and she won! I knew she had suffered but I had no idea at the time just how much. No one who has not been through it can imagine how awful it is--both for the patient and for those who love her. But, sadly, I found out what it is like.

In 1994, my husband Jim was diagnosed with Stage IV stomach cancer. He had been complaining of stomach pain and difficulty swallowing for months, but the doctor had told him he had "acid reflux" and recommended Mylanta. Finally, we changed doctors and were sent for diagnosis in Pittsburgh. When

94

they said "inoperable cancer," we were stunned and scared and very unsure about what to do. Shortly after his diagnosis, Patsy came to town. She was starting to grow back the hair she had lost during her chemotherapy treatments (*see color photo 3*). But she came to our house *without* her wig to give Jim a "pep" talk. She showed him that she had survived and gave him hope that he, too, could conquer it. That night she convinced him to have the treatments that I believe extended his life a few months. She sent cards and letters and a whole box of inspirational books that she had been given over the course of her illness. And she sent back the AMY bear to watch over Jim. She quoted Bible verses and was our "light" to keep going. "Patsy made it; so can we!" We said it all the time; and we believed it.

I also found out what Patsy must have suffered. And I realized how her family must have suffered to watch her struggle. Jim also had the chemotherapy treatments and resulting blood transfusions. It was a 24-hour-a-day challenge and he fought each minute of each day. He never complained. He said, "If it is killing the good cells, then it must be killing the bad cells." We tried infusions of vitamin C and every "alternative" cure we could find; we changed our diet and he spent hours working on mental immuno-therapy. And he outlived all expectations. He beat back the tumors for months and attended a Thanksgiving family reunion that no one expected him to see. But he finally couldn't fight anymore.

Jim died in March of 1995, at the age of forty-five and the pain is still enormous. He left two sons and many friends and family members who miss him more than words can tell. But I do thank Patsy for giving him hope--that's the way he wanted to fight, believing right until the end that he could win. And I think he almost did. I know it wasn't easy for her. It probably wasn't healthy for her to think about someone else losing the battle. But she loved Jim and he loved her and I love her because she is as good a person as I have ever known.

Katie Couric (of the "Today" show) recently lost her husband to cancer; he was forty-two. I thought she seemed to be coping pretty well; she was back at work each morning, smiling and doing a great job. But I read parts of a speech she gave, and I realized that the premature loss of someone you love creates a universal bond of tears and suffering that no one can escape. Katie Couric said, "Now I know the sheer terror of living with a life-threatening illness and being a part of that life every single day." She asked the question we all ask, "How do you go on when fate delivers such a crushing blow that it causes permanent damage to your heart?"

I had kept all of Jim's get-well cards and the sympathy cards we received after he died. I recently sorted through them as I forced myself to throw away some of the painful memories. I found a note that Patsy had written me a couple of weeks after Jim's death. She was referring to their loss of Beth when she wrote to me, "*. . .You must take comfort in knowing that you did everything humanly possible for Jim. . .I'm sure you are blessed with many wonderful friends and family members who are helping you through this. They will never fill the gap left behind but I'm sure will be of great support. . .All I can say is that time will help. When (Beth) was killed 3 years ago, it was devastating. The hurt never goes away--but time makes living more tolerable. There is never a day that goes by that you don't think about the person you've lost--you don't want to stop remembering. All you have left are the fond remembrances. Treasure them. I've tried to find some comfort from the Bible and all I can seem to absorb is that there must be 'a purpose under heaven' for everything. I guess we won't possibly understand the purpose until we get there. Our only consolation when we lost Beth was that we would meet again in our 'eternal reunion'. Her marker bears this verse. John and I both believe it--it is the only thing that keeps it bearable. I know that where there is love there will be this eternal reunion. . .*"

I am trying to find the faith and the strength that Patsy and John seem to have, but it isn't easy. I know it must comfort them that they know in their hearts that Beth and JonBenét are together.

After eight wrenching chemotherapy sessions, Patsy's cancer was gone. What a miracle! Everyone who knows and loves Patsy felt that our prayers were answered. But Patsy was more than just a survivor; she was an inspiration to others--physically, emotionally and spiritually. When Patsy went back for checkups at NIH, she spoke to support groups to give encouragement and tell them to never, ever give up hope. Patsy once asked her nurse (after some of the people in her cancer study had died), "Why do you do this work?" And the nurse answered, "Because of people like you. When we are successful and even one person lives and has their life restored, it makes it all worthwhile." And Patsy continues to help anyone who needs comfort and support and advice. She can't help but give and give and give; that's just how she is.

One of the women who shared this cancer experience with Patsy was named Barbara. She tells of their struggle:

Barbara's story:

"I first met Patsy at the National Cancer Institute, National Institutes of Health (NIH) in September, 1993. We had both been diagnosed with ovarian cancer that summer, Patsy was Stage IV, I was Stage III C. We were fortunate to be accepted into the NIH Protocol for Ovarian Cancer Research. Patsy knew one of the people I worked with at the Resolution Trust Corporation who had told her to look for me as I was also a patient at NIH and didn't have any family in the DC area. We were roommates several times, and instant friends.

"She was a favorite of everyone. Whenever she saw you, her first concern and question was "How are you doing?" She put everyone at ease; no one was a stranger. I feel like the phrase "never met a stranger" was coined for people like her. Her love of people and life shines out of her. Patsy is what I consider to be a good person and a wonderful friend. For instance, she read a book that gave her consolation, was inspirational to her and answered some of the questions that people in our situation asked ourselves every minute of the day. She thought it would help, so she ordered several dozen and gave them to other cancer patients in the hope that the book would also help them.

"There was another friend, Vicki Chabol, who unfortunately passed away this past New Years. The three of us would try to get our appointment times at the same time. We would go have lunch together and catch up on what had been happening. It was usually the last meal we would be able to digest for several days. During treatment we were there for five (5) days every 21 days. Patsy and I went into remission, but Vicki had to continue treatment for several months after we finished ours. We gave each other support, it was like we were family. We could always joke with each other about our wigs (talk about bad hair days) and other things that only another cancer patient could truly appreciate. They were both there for me when my cancer

came back for the second time.

"Patsy was always talking about John and her children. She was so proud of them. I saw them as a family several times; I went to Boulder, and they came to Phoenix. The children I saw were both loved and loving and certainly behaved like normal children. They played with their friends and got messy just like all children do. She talked about Burke and his piano recitals and JonBenét. One November she told me about JonBenét and how they had just been to New York with her mom and sisters. Patsy was laughing about JonBenét. It seems she had seen a couple of Broadway shows, been ice skating at Rockefeller Center, but the highlight for JonBenét was the Rockettes. She told Patsy she wanted to be a Rockette when she grew up. A month later she was gone. What a tragedy for us all. She was a bright, beautiful and loving child.

The thought that anyone could ever think that Patsy would ever harm any one, or let any one who had harmed someone she loved go unpunished is ludicrous. I sent the following poem to Patsy. It was written by Barbara English of Arizona."

The love of a friend
is a powerful prayer
for it carries hope
and heals despair.

The hug of a friend
helps a heart to mend
it lessens the load
and speaks louder than words
restoring peace
to a hurting soul.

Peace and love Patsy,
Barbara K. Sanders
"Colonel Barbara"

This painful chapter of Patsy's life closes like the others, with no hidden secrets, no events that show a sinister side and nothing that happened to change her from the generous, loving person she has always been.

September 1985, Patsy and John with Melinda, John Andrew and Beth. Beth was killed in an auto accident in 1992.

Patsy often thanked my husband, Jim, for his patience the summer we worked every day on her preparation for the Miss America pageant. He was very proud of her. She jokingly called him "dad". Picture from 1977.

Chapter Eight:
Family Life
in Boulder and Michigan

Friends and family had always been very important to Patsy, but after the struggle with cancer, they became even more so. She wanted to find ways to bring the family together more often and made sure she found time to spend with her special friends.

Here is cousin Debbie's account of some happy family times A.C. (after cancer):

"Patsy planned two family reunions at the lake in Michigan, one in the summer of 1995 and one in the summer of 1996. I have vivid memories from both.

"In one invitation, Patsy suggested we should each prepare an act for the 'family talent show.' I did a very amateur rendition of the 'Itsy Bitsy Spider.' (Remember, I didn't have the singing talent in the family.) Pam and I did a skit where she sang and moved her arms and I was the legs trying to keep beat to the music. I remember that John did an adorable comedy act with Burke; JonBenét and her cousin did a little song and dance number. They loved to do the Macarena--over and over again. Just ask them--or they would show you anyway! Patsy sang along with a record (Patsy Cline's, I think). It was a special family time, just as Patsy had wanted.

"In the summer of 1996, the reunion was held in August and we celebrated JonBenét's birthday. The main thing she wanted that year was an American Girl doll named Samantha. When she opened the box, with Burkey's help, she said, 'Oh, my doll,' and hugged and hugged her new baby (see photo). This

picture that I took that day is one I haven't even shown to Patsy yet. It is still too painful.

"This is how I knew her best--dressed in blue jean shorts, sandals, a T-shirt and a pony tail. JonniB on her 6th birthday was an ordinary and wonderful little angel with her favorite doll, her puppy Jacque, and her loving family.

"The birthday doll had a book that came with it. When I was reading the book to JonBenét one night as she got ready for bed, we came to the part about the little girl giving up her favorite doll to a sick child. I cried and JonBenét cried. She was a bright, loving and very giving child. She would understand a story like this, even at her age, and she seemed to want everyone to be happy. It's hard to explain how extraordinary she was; you just had to know her.

"JonBenét wanted to have a pajama party--so Grandma, Aunts, Mom and Cousins all gathered in the living room for the night. One of the games we played was something that JonBenét thought of. We each pretended to be a different animal in a pet shop. I was a parrot; Grandma Nedra was a dog; there was an alligator, a kitty cat and a rabbit. We giggled and we laughed and we told funny stories in our animal voices and we made our animal sounds. I wish we had a video tape! It's hard to imagine acting so silly, but it's just one more time that I can't get out of my mind.

"I next saw Patsy when I was invited to Boulder for her surprise 40th Birthday party. Even though Patsy's birthday wasn't until December, John had decided to have the party in November because of the busy holidays coming up. He left the planning to two of Patsy's friends; it was a grand party. We had dinner at the Brown Palace Hotel in Denver, followed with a band, dancing and a fellow who came dressed up like Miss America and did a comedy routine about Patsy's life and accomplishments. It was very uplifting because we were all so thankful that she was still here and able to celebrate her 40th birthday.

"The morning after the party, I remember all of us being in one bed and talking 'girl talk.' There was Patsy, Pam, Paulette, Melinda, JonBenét and myself. We giggled and talked about the party, how great it was to be together and what was happening in our lives. Patsy talked about her anticipated trip to New York City with JonBenét and other friends and their daughters. They *called it the 'mother-daughter' trip.*

"JonBenét was special. She enjoyed her friends and toys, but she also enjoyed being with her mom and family. She never seemed to whine or want all of the attention like children of that age might do. She listened and even joined in the conversation and seemed content just to be with the big girls and we loved having her with us.

"JonBenét once wrapped her arms around my leg and started talking to me and then realized, 'You're not my mommy.' I guess it was because Patsy and I look so much alike. I didn't have a daughter and I always felt a very special bond with her. I called her 'JonniB,' as did most of the family. JonBenét called me Aunt Debbie and Pam and Polly jokingly reminded her, 'No, Debbie is your cousin, not your aunt.' But JonBenét told them with what made logical sense to her, 'Aunts are big and Cousins are little, so Debbie must be my Aunt!'

"John Ramsey was a gentle father. Patsy was a patient mother. I never saw either of them yell or raise a hand to their children. Both parents hugged their children and weren't afraid to show or express affection with names like 'sweetie.' When the kids did something wrong, Patsy would sit down and talk about it. She would say quietly but firmly, 'We don't do that.' And then she would explain why not. I don't remember either child having a temper tantrum. They weren't perfect, of course. Burke was aggravated when JonBenét would get in front of the television and she would pester him like siblings do, but he never really got mad and you could tell he really cared for her. As I think back over all of the times I spent with them, they seemed to be remarkably well-behaved and happy children. And they certainly were well-loved! JonniB was easy-going like her mom and she was so sweet that it made you want to give her anything she wanted. There wasn't much she didn't get, but she wasn't spoiled or demanding. She was a wonderful child and I really loved her a lot; we all did!"

signed: Debbie

It seems that everyone I speak with has the same sincere, unwavering belief in Patsy and John. As I said, I didn't have much contact with them while they lived in Boulder. But I spoke with one of their best friends from there. Her name is Susan Stine. Patsy and Susan met when their sons Doug and

Burke were in the same kindergarten class. Patsy has previously told me how much she admires Susan--her education, her intelligence and her innovative ideas. And as I talked to Susan about contributing to this book I found out that the feelings were mutual. Susan told me how much she admired Patsy--as an enthusiastic organizer, as a mother and as a cancer survivor. Their friendship is much more than just two "school moms."

Patsy told me that, after the tragedy, Susan's compassion was one of the things that helped her through the darkest times. *"There was a time when I was nothing but a basket case,"* Patsy remembers. *"Susan took care of me--almost like a mother. There were days I could hardly function and she helped me with everything from getting dressed to taking care of Burke. I'll always appreciate her loving support."* Susan knows Patsy well and passionately believes in her goodness.

Here are some of Susan's memories:

"I first met Patsy when our boys were in kindergarten (1992-1993). Patsy was the perfect home room mother--always volunteering to head the fund-raisers and plan the children's activities. I watched Patsy pour tremendous energy and talent into everything she did--from helping kids with their lessons to decorating for classroom parties. As I grew to know her, I learned more and more about what a wonderfully generous person she is. Here's a small example:

"One year, the school decided to have a family party based on a western theme. This was to be not only a fund-raiser, but also was to build community spirit. Patsy took on a major responsibility, wanting to make this something really special for the children. Patsy invited Burke's class and their parents to her home to make preparations. This included painting scenery and making props. What a wonderful, memorable (and messy!) afternoon. One of Patsy's biggest talents is her organization. She had all of the materials ready for the day--paint and cardboard and fabric and ribbon, etc. And she didn't just supervise. She pitched in and did the hard work--painting, cutting, glueing and anything else that needed to be done.

"Burke's job was making lemonade and serving cookies.

Of course the floor was a sticky mess--but Patsy didn't seem to care a bit. John was there, too, and seemed happy to open his house to this noisy, messy group. He obviously enjoyed this beehive of activity as he talked and laughed with the children. This was a home full of love and laughter, welcoming everyone who entered it. No one was a stranger to Patsy and John.

"When one of our friends turned 40, Patsy helped the friend's husband plan a surprise party. Again, Patsy planned each detail carefully and made this an extraordinary occasion. She filled her house with yellow roses, our friend's favorite. Patsy included things that our friend loved--like Texas line dancing and a Bar-B-Q. Patsy and John opened their home to the birthday girl's friends from church, school and the neighborhood, many of whom the Ramseys didn't even know. It was just another example of Patsy's ability to graciously make her friend's special occasion memorable and bring her happiness.

"I work in education and one of the things I most admired about Patsy was her commitment to her children's education. When our boys were in second grade, the Boulder school district set up several new schools, each with a particular 'focus.' Together we decided to look at one school in particular which adopted the Core Knowledge Curriculum. We attended an Open House and were impressed. We decided to go to another town, Fort Collins, about two hours from Boulder, to see a school like this in operation. Patsy wanted to see exactly what Burke would be studying and find out how the program actually worked.

"When we arrived at the school, I was amazed that Patsy had researched the curriculum and had questions already prepared to ask the teachers. She said she wanted to thoroughly understand the program so she and John could decide if it was what they thought would be best for Burke. We had talked about stopping at a big mall on the way home to do a little shopping, but we spent all day at the school and had no time for the mall. I should have known that Patsy wouldn't leave until she had looked into every aspect of something as important as a school curriculum for her son.

"Patsy is pretty, but I never thought of her as vain. I remember one particular evening at the lake when Patsy had been playing with the kids and relaxing, winding down from a family reunion with a house full of relatives. She was in shorts and had no makeup on. My husband and I had dinner reserva-

tions and we asked Patsy if they'd like to go. 'Sure, I'll get ready right away,' she said. The reservations were in less than a half-hour and the restaurant was in the next town, so I thought we should call and let the restaurant know we'd probably be late. But Patsy appeared in what couldn't have been more than 5 minutes--dressed and ready to go. I envied her ability to get ready so fast and look so good! She told us, 'I can get ready for any occasion in under 10 minutes. With all of the things I have to do in a day, I have to be able to move quickly.' She cared about looking her best, but it was far from her top priority. She had learned from her struggle with cancer how unimportant outward appearances are.

"Speaking of lack of vanity, I remember seeing her at school and home without any hair and I was inspired by her energy and enthusiasm. Chemotherapy treatments had rendered her bald, and she had wigs that she sometimes wore. But she said they were hot and uncomfortable and that she didn't care what she looked like. And she knew the children would accept her for what she was like on the inside, not what she looked like on the outside.

"One of the most vivid memories I have is of an afternoon at the beach with Patsy and the kids. We were in Michigan; the Ramseys were there for summer vacation and we had gone back to visit the places where my husband and I grew up.

"You should see the car that they drive in Michigan; it's a huge 1984 Cadillac DeVille that Patsy's parents gave to them. This colossal vehicle was the perfect car for a trip to the beach. We packed folding chairs, boogie boards, floats, toys, towels, and food for the 5-minute trip.

"As the kids took their swim toys and raced into the water, Patsy and I put our chairs in the sand to relax and watch the children play. I had never really talked to Patsy much about her cancer. When she was sick, I was at work every day and she spent a lot of time at home with her family. Visitors were restricted because of the possibility of giving her infections that could be life-threatening. Until that afternoon, I had not realized how serious her illness was nor how painful her recovery. Most of our friendship has grown after she finished her treatments.

"Patsy told me of her family's history of ovarian cancer, how her older relatives had not seen the connections between illnesses that the women suffered, in many cases not realizing *even when they died that it was probably ovarian cancer. It has one of the highest mortality rates of all cancers. She told me how she had gone to doctors complaining of a shoulder pain that they couldn't seem to trace to anything. Once she'd had a CAT scan of her upper body, but it had ended just above where the cancer was, so it was not detected. By the time her stomach was swollen with cancer and she went to the hospital, they found out that her cancer was already in Stage IV, the most severe level of all. It's the same kind that Gilda Radner had. I had read Gilda's book about her terrible experience.*

"We talked about her entry into the experimental treatment program at the National Institutes of Health. I knew that to subject oneself to these kinds of medical protocols, your illness has to be very desperate. It's a last resort because no one knows what will work. I realized as she told me of her rigorous treatments and adverse physical reactions, that she must have suffered a great deal. And yet she had done what she could to keep her family's life as normal as it could be. Her children were so well-adjusted and happy. They were the joy of her and John's lives and the reason she struggled through the hell of her chemotherapy, the terrible weeks and months of pain, knowing that the odds of survival were very slim. (Since that summer day, I have learned that many of the women who were in the NIH experimental treatment with Patsy have died. Patsy, thank God, remains free of symptoms.)

"Patsy is always ready to help those who face the same diagnosis. People contact her all the time for advice on who to see about their illness and how to endure it. Locally, she has helped a number of friends (and friends of friends) who have had to cope with cancer in their families. Even after JonBenét's death, people would call or write to get help from her and she would rise above her own sorrow to get them connected to the right people. I have read some of these letters and it still amazes me how much of herself Patsy is willing to give to others.

"I was struck that day at the beach by her attitude. I think I would have been angry and resentful if this had happened to me--the lonely months in agony, not knowing whether all of the treatments would help or not, not knowing whether any day might be the last with my family. I could imagine how depressed I would have been. I was in awe of Patsy for her ability to call on her faith, her positive attitude and her inner strength.

I had no idea on that beautiful summer day how much more she would have to endure. As I watched my son playing with Burke and JonBenét, I said a little prayer that he would be safe and that I would be with him for a long time. I wish I had said one for Patsy that day, too.

"I have known Patsy before, during and after her horrible loss. I have seen her in situations from profound happiness to the depths of grief and I know what a wonderful human being she is. I have watched Patsy and John endure the worst kind of cruelty imaginable, and yet their faith in God and each other never waivers, and their love for their family pulls them through. They have persevered with a dignity and courage that is seldom seen in our world. I am proud to be their friend; I will always be their friend."

signed: Susan Stine

Linda Mason first met the Ramseys when they bought a summer home in Charlevoix, Michigan. She, like so many others, talked at length about what a wonderful family life the Ramseys shared. It was heartwarming to me as I wrote this book to see the great number of Patsy's friends who not only loved her, but wanted to strongly and publicly proclaim their faith in her.

Linda's Story:

"I had gone out of town to spend Christmas 1996 at my sister's home. When I checked my answering machine, I heard a message that something had happened to JonBenét. I knew the Ramseys were supposed to be in Charlevoix that day, so I assumed JonBenét had had an accident. Was she hit by a car? When I finally reached a neighbor who told me JonBenét had been killed, I was absolutely stunned--beyond belief! As I watched events unfold on the news, I remember thinking, 'It has to be someone who knew the family and knew the house!'

"I couldn't help but remember over and over again the 2 weeks I had spent with the Ramseys at their home in Boulder just a couple of months before, in late October. I had slept next to JonBenét's room, in the guest room near the spiral staircase. Each morning Patsy would be the first to get up and I would hear her going down that staircase to start the coffee. She would

come back upstairs, wake the children and help them get ready for school. After breakfast, she would take her turn carpooling.

"But no matter where we were or what we were doing in the afternoon, Patsy was always back to greet her children after school. And she didn't just wait in the line. She'd get out of the car, walk up to meet them, give them a big hug and kiss and ask, 'How was your day?' Then there was usually an activity for the children–French lessons which they seemed to really like, sports, dance or swim class. They were very active kids and I remember thinking how wonderful it was that Patsy was so interested and involved with their lives.

"And every evening the family ate together. Even when we went out to dinner, it was John and Patsy and JonBenét and Burke together. . .a family time. They discussed the day's activities. After dinner, Mom made sure that the homework was done. At night Patsy tucked JonBenét into bed and read her a story. Sound like a typical family life? It was. And the love and affection that these parents had for their children was obvious.

"For some reason, I remember the dog. I had been at the Ramseys' house for a couple of days when I noticed their dog for the first time. It seems that it had two homes. It ran freely between the Ramseys and the house across the street. And children came freely into the home to play, running through the house, laughing. Neighbors would stop by. Everyone seemed welcome. It was just wonderful to be in this home.

"When I saw the big emphasis that was made by the press about JonBenét's pageants, I was surprised. I knew she had entered her first contest in Michigan as a summertime fun activity. JonBenét was almost 5 and had never been in something like this before so they were surprised and pleased when she won. But it was just for fun. They would be just as pleased if Burke's ball team won a playoff game.

"Once I walked into their living room and saw JonBenét on Patsy's lap. They were talking about a contest that JonBenét had been in and I asked her, 'How did you do?' She didn't answer me but looked shyly at her mom. Finally, when Patsy encouraged her to answer, she said simply, 'I won,' and then hopped down and went outside to play. I had no idea until later that it was the Little Miss Colorado Pageant. Other than that one instance, in all the time I've known them and have been in their home, I have never heard any mention of pageants or competi-

*tion. It just wasn't a focal point of JonBenét life and I hate that
it has become a focal point of her death.*

*"I remember the little things. Two years ago I got a present
from Patsy with a birthday note from JonBenét. The present was
fragrances for the bath and it still sits on a tray in my bathroom.
Patsy was always doing special little things for other people and
she taught JonBenét to be just as thoughtful. I think of all of the
good times we have shared and it is very, very sad that something so horrible has happened to people who are so good. Patsy
is just a joy to be around! She is one of the most energetic, enthusiastic, loving people I have ever spent time with.*

*"I never would have expected that someday I would have
to put on paper a denial about people who are so special. But I
say it without reservation: Never, never, ever, ever has there been
the slightest thought in my mind--in any way, shape or form--
that John or Patsy could have been involved with their child's
death. Absolutely no way!"*

signed: Linda Mason

And so, as we end this chapter of Patsy's life before her
daughter was killed, we see again that she was a good friend, a
good mom, a good wife, a good person. Again, there are no questions, no doubts. There are no secret stories; there are no hints
of some other, darker side of Patsy. She was the same wonderful person from the day she was born until the day of the tragedy. She is still the same wonderful person, only now she has to
cope with the ultimate sadness.

This book has been about seeing Patsy's life from all
sides and knowing that any way you look at her, you will find
goodness clear to the soul. As friend after friend are willing to
sign their names on strong, unequivocal statements of belief in
Patsy's innocence, we know that it is true.

JonBenét hugging new "Samantha" doll at her sixth birthday party in Michigan, August 1996.

Patsy with JonBenét and Burke. Patsy helped organize a Western Theme Party for the elementary school.

After living in Atlanta, the Ramsey children enjoyed the Colorado snowfalls. They liked to build snowmen. JonBenét was learning to ski.

The family loves to spend time at the lake in Michigan--John and Patsy.

Patsy clowns for the camera during "happier days" at the lake.

JonBenét liked to drive the pontoon boat and skip rocks on the lake.

Chapter Nine:
After JonBenét

When I heard about JonBenét's death, I knew I had to see to Patsy, so I took a plane to Atlanta for the funeral. I arrived early at the church but the family was already there, gathered in a sitting room. They all looked like they were in shock and were just "going through the motions". I knew that feeling only too well. Patsy could hardly stand but she kept trying to get up to hug people. She looked so small and wounded, leaning on someone else's arm. I don't remember what we talked about--it's the kind of meaningless conversation people have to make at times like this. They asked about what song might be appropriate for the organist to play, and I suggested "Let There Be Peace On Earth" which we had played at my husband Jim's funeral.

I hurt for Patsy; I hurt for John; I hurt for Nedra and Don and Pam and Polly and the rest of the family. And I hurt for me--I let out some of the grief I had been storing since I lost Jim. I had not gone to a grief recovery group yet or even spoken at length to anyone about it. I had held it inside and suddenly I faced it. When Patsy asked me, "Do you think Jim and JonBenét are together?", I just about lost my composure completely. I wanted to help and I realized that, of course, there was absolutely nothing I could do.

During the funeral, I sat in the row behind Patsy and John and I could not look at them without crying. They had already closed the casket when I first walked into the sanctuary and I was just as glad because I was pretty shaky. I don't remember anything about the actual service; it's like a haze. It's hard to describe the feeling--the word "heavy" is one that comes to mind. Your heart and even your physical body seem like there are weights attached. I think that anyone who has lost a loved one suddenly probably knows what I am talking about. It seems like nothing is real; you want to stop time and say, "Wait a minute; this isn't right." You mumble things that are meant to comfort and may even smile a little and then wonder what you said or why you smiled.

JonBenét's sister and brothers were there. And the aunts and cousins and so many, many friends. I realized how far the ripples of this crime had reached, and how deep. It affected so many lives and caused so much pain. I know God says we are to forgive even the worst sinner. I don't know if I could have the faith to even begin to forgive the monster who caused all of this pain.

I rode with Patsy's cousin Debbie to the cemetery and I remember that reporters and cameramen were standing across the street. I thought how strange it was that they were there and how awful it was that they couldn't leave the family alone. But I didn't imagine for one second that they would question whether Patsy and John had something to do with it. That would never have crossed my mind.

I went back to Patsy's parents' house where the whole family was staying. They insisted I stay with them that night, so I just tried to help by fixing food, making beds, etc. I sat with Burke who was playing Nintendo games and I watched a movie with him--I think it was *Star Wars*. I read to Nedra from an inspirational book I had taken with me. It was an awful time. There aren't words to describe how distraught and devastated the whole family was. The phone rang and rang and no one wanted to answer. It seemed like we'd fix food and then no one was hungry. Now that the funeral was over, what was there to do? It was like everyone was moving in slow motion. Patsy cried. John paced back and forth, back and forth in his stocking feet. Nedra curled up on the bed and Don tried to calm her when she got hysterical, but he was crying, too. We all cried. Pam and Debbie and I talked a little about how awful it was that whoever did this may have been someone John and Patsy knew. It was so very painful to watch them suffer.

I had brought back the AMY bear for Patsy. When I gave it to her, she just hugged it to her chest and actually fell on her knees on the floor and cried and said, "Linda, they killed my baby." I couldn't think of anything at all to say that made any sense. Later, we talked a little about the past. But I knew the conversation wasn't registering. I saw the anguish, the numbness, the glazed eyes full of disbelief and crushing pain. And I recognized those emotions because I had gone through them, too, with the loss of my husband. But, as bad as my loss had been, I did have time to prepare. Patsy had the added burden of the sudden, unexpected, unexplained, unbelievable death. She was talking but not really focusing. I think she really was in shock and I assume she was also medicated. I know there are people who think that Patsy might have had something to do with this. Those people have not seen her grief; they haven't heard her sobs.

The next day, we talked and cried together again. She kept saying again, "They killed my baby; they killed my baby!" And she kept asking, "why?" I didn't have an answer and didn't know any words to say to help. All of the normal things like "You have to be strong for Burke" and "God has a plan" and "You will get through this" just didn't seem like enough. Somehow we started talking about a "mission". Patsy said that maybe there was something she could do to make JonBenét's life mean more. Maybe there was a cause that she could get involved with or a way to do something special in the name of JonBenét. I told her to hang on to that thought and make that her reason for getting up each day. I told her that she didn't have to start that week or even that year. But when she was ready, sometime in the future, she and John and the whole family and even friends could and would make a difference in the name of JonBenét. It was something that seemed to give her some peace. Several times since that conversation, she has said to me, 'Let's talk about the mission." I know they have founded the JonBenét Ramsey Children's Foundation and I know that someday they will make a difference. I hope I can help.

Patsy visited us last October. She had flown with her mother to Pittsburgh to see one of the women who was in the cancer treatment program with her. Vicki Chabol wasn't doing well and Patsy felt she just had to go see her--to pray for her. (In December, I called Vicki to see if she wanted to contribute her thoughts to this book. She could hardly speak; she was weak and obviously in pain. I told her not to strain herself to talk and that I would call later. She said in a voice I could hardly hear, "But I want to help. I want to talk about how good Patsy is." Then she started coughing and couldn't continue. It sounded like she could hardly breathe. I tried to say something comforting and I got off the phone quickly. Vicki died on New Year's Day and we never had a chance to speak again. But she wanted to add her support for Patsy so I am putting her name in this book as a memorial tribute to her. In her darkest hour, Vicki cared enough about her friend Patsy to want to help her. She, too, knew what a wonderful person Patsy is.)

After their visit to see Vicki, Patsy and her mother stopped in Morgantown to visit West Virginia University. They went by Patsy's old sorority house and walked through the journalism school halls. Then they came to Parkersburg and spent four days at my house. We had lunch with some old friends; we attended a high school football game to watch her former drill team perform; she helped her uncle with some home repairs; she visited with relatives; she bought some of my son's baseball cards for Burke. I think it was nice for her to be surrounded by people who love her and believe in her and remember better times.

On Sunday, we attended the church where Patsy and her family had gone when they lived here. Since I was not a member of that church, I asked my friend Karen to save us seats. When we went to sit down, Nedra said that it was the same pew where her family sat so many years ago. And when the people in front of us turned around to say hello, they were the same people who had sat in front of Patsy's family back then. The regular minister was off that day and the substitute was the father of one of Pam's best childhood friends. It seemed very comforting. I took a picture of Patsy with Reverend Harden and when it was developed, there was a light shining on Patsy (*see color photo 8*). I like to think that God is taking care of her.

The minister introduced Patsy and Nedra and prayed for them. He asked Patsy if she wanted to say a few words so she went to the pulpit and spoke to the congregation. She used the Bible verse from Corinthians 1:13 which says "and so abideth faith, hope and love, but the greatest of these is love." She said that she continued to have faith in God because without that, life was meaningless. She talked about hope of seeing JonBenét again someday and that being the reason to go on. And she thanked others for their love and support. She said it a lot better than I am repeating here; it came from her heart.

I had told one of Patsy's friends that she and her mom

would be coming and they had arranged a small reception in the church hall for them after the service. Again, it was a gathering of people who believe in Patsy and wanted to help her. They knew that "cookies and punch" are just tokens of support and love and yet it was a chance to do something, however small, to say to Patsy and her mom that their old friends and neighbors are still here to lean on.

While she was here, we had long conversations--trying to understand why JonBenét and Jim had to be taken so soon. At one point we were talking about raising our sons and I said that sometimes my boys don't understand my rules and question why they have to do something. I answer as my parents answered my same questions and all parents answer their children: "I'm the mother; that's why. You may not understand now, but someday you will know why." Then, at the same moment, Patsy and I said, "I'm the Father, that's why". We talked about being God's children and asking Him why and maybe He has to give us the same answer that we give our children. He loves us like we love our children and He hates to see us suffer, but He knows that someday we will understand. It was comforting to both Patsy and I as we pondered this "new" thought. After her visit, I found she had left a little angel doll, with blond hair in pigtails; I put it next to Jim's picture on my dresser.

I had heard Bill Cosby recently say, "God, too, knows the pain of losing a child. God didn't give our son to us, but just loaned him to us for a while." I told this to Patsy along with things I had been learning in my grief recovery group. Later, on a visit to Atlanta, Patsy and I again had conversations about JonBenét and Jim. And, at one point, we talked about something that Patsy had been thinking about. Although God did suffer the loss of a child, He knew His child was coming home to Him. Jesus' mother Mary also suffered, and she had faith, but she was left behind. Patsy has great faith and I know it helps her keep going each day. But she is the one left behind. Although I can understand some of her pain, I can't imagine how she deals with the media and suspicions and failure to find the person who did this. I think at times she just has to block it all out of her mind and just live day-to-day with her routines.

One night when Patsy and I were talking on the phone, she said something that really hit me hard. She had called around ten o'clock at night and seemed very "down." In the middle of a conversation about something else, Patsy suddenly changed the subject and talked about how, earlier that day, she had been waiting for Burke in the car pool line after school and was listening to the radio. The announcer said something about a special news conference in Boulder and that John and Patsy Ramsey were still under the umbrella of suspicion. "It just isn't real; it's like an out-of-body experience," she said. "It's like they are talking about someone else. How could this be happening?" Can you imagine--waiting for your son to come out of school and hearing someone say on the radio that you are a suspect in the murder of your daughter? I don't know how she can bear it.

After the tragedy, Patsy could not go back to the house in Boulder where they found JonBenét. She and John and Burke stayed with friends in Boulder while Burke finished his school year and then they moved back to Atlanta where their families live. I was recently in Atlanta and spent some time at her house. Patsy spends her days doing what moms do. She is a team mother for Burke's baseball team; she helps him with school projects. John takes Burke camping with the Boy Scouts. They see Patsy's sisters and parents and John's brother and family often. Patsy and John go to their Sunday School class. He plays ball with the dog and she does the laundry. He works at the computer; she recently hand-painted glasses for Melinda's wedding shower. It all seems so normal--except for the painful loss and the ridiculous cloud hanging over their heads.

This book was dedicated to all of those who have lost a loved one suddenly or too soon. You know the devastating feelings. You know the pain. Can you imagine the added burden of having people suspect you had something to do with that loss? It's beyond what anyone should have to endure. The media treats them like they are "things" to be discussed and dissected. They are real people with real feelings and real pain. And it's time that we realize how we torture innocent people in the name of our "right to know".

Her family suffers, too. Her parents not only grieve for the loss of their granddaughter, but they endure the pain of seeing their daughter and son-in-law suffer. Her sisters mourn the loss of their niece and they also agonize over the pain their sister must live with. And they hurt for John's suffering. And for Burke.

122

And their friends are frustrated as month after month goes by with no conclusion to this travesty. We want to help and there is so little that we can do. We can pray. We can offer words of encouragement. And we can write this book to let Patsy and John know we stand behind them, we believe in them and we are not afraid to tell the world how much we love them. And we can let the world know that we miss JonBenét. No one could say it better than in this letter which was written by a family which is friends with the Ramseys:

Dear JonBenét,

We miss you. We miss your silly smile and grass-stained knees. We miss your flag dance routines and the way you would plead for fireworks after dark. We miss playing on the swing set and picking blueberries by the driveway. We miss riding decorated bikes, swimming in the pool and swinging on sky chairs. We miss going to the beach to watch the sunset and skipping rocks in Lake Michigan. We miss sliding down the hill in cardboard box cars after spending hours decorating them with crayons and markers. We miss roasting hotdogs and marshmallows with you in the fire pit. Sister Socks, our cat, misses you too.

Over the last year and a half, I have experienced so many unbelievable things. I have had to explain to Taylor and Mikaela why they constantly see pictures of you and your parents at the grocery store check out line. They wonder why you are always shown dressed up like a beautiful doll, not as they knew you, just one of the gang. I have had to sadly reply that I don't know how someone could do this. Momma just doesn't know the answer.

I have had to confront people stopping, staring and photographing our friend's house, questioning why it is suddenly OK to invade someone's right to privacy. They fail to put this into perspective, to try to imagine the horror of the situation your parents have been put in. I am certain that you are in a better place, but you must be sad that your loved ones have been left in such a cruel world. I watch Mikaela play dolls in your room and wonder why she has to talk to you in a photograph as if you were there. You should be there.

I am so proud of your parents and your brother Burke. They have somehow managed to be strong, to find a new direction for the family. You are still a vital part of everything they

123

do. Your smiling face is there, in pictures that remind them of your full and happy life, regardless of how short it was. You have not been forgotten or pushed out of sight, a memory too painful to acknowledge each day. Instead, you are everywhere that I look. You grin in a snow suit, your cheeks rosy and warm. You stand in a pose, thrilled to dress up like a big girl, like your mom, whom you adore. You drive the pontoon boat on a blue sky day with your golden arms wet from the spray. All of this reminds me of how lucky you were. You were part of a family that not only loved you, but were able to provide you with the things that most of us only wish for.

You were as we remember you, a normal, happy, healthy little girl. You are still someone we love and miss each day.

Love,
The Witthoefts
(Shelly and A.J.,
Taylor and Mikaela)

Patsy with childhood friends who dropped by to offer support.

Patsy buys baseball cards for Burke from Mark McLean, October 1997.

Patsy Ramsey and Linda McLean have been friends for twenty-five years.

Conclusion:
Thoughts About the Murder

It's hard for me to even write the word "murder," let alone think so much about it, but there are some things I just have to say. Patsy and I haven't talked much about specifics. But I have watched television shows and I have read some articles in the more "reputable" magazines and newspapers. I have heard a lot of information that may or may not be completely accurate, but I think I know from these sources the basic facts.

Sometimes it all just swirls around in my head and I try to make some sense of it. I taught debate at our local high school; maybe it's the "debater" in me that is searching for logic, that tries to put the pieces of the puzzle together.

But I always come to the obvious conclusion that it makes absolutely no sense to suspect Patsy and John. The facts that I have heard plus a little common sense will not allow a rational person to really believe that they were involved.

I hesitated to write this chapter because it sounds like I am trying to play lawyer or detective--and I certainly am not. I know that the lawyers and investigators and detectives are doing their jobs and hopefully they will eventually be successful in finding the truth.

But I finally decided that I cannot let this book be published without "saying my piece". I know the others who spoke in this book probably agree with me, but we didn't collaborate on this last chapter. These are my thoughts; these are my conclusions. It's just Linda shouting: "It doesn't make any sense!"

I don't know exactly what the Ramseys did on Christmas Day, 1996. I imagine they did what most of us did—opened presents and called family members. Patsy and John are very

127

religious so maybe they went to church or read the story of the Christ child. John and Patsy probably cleaned up the wrapping paper as Burke and JonBenét played with their new toys. That was private family time, but we can all picture it.

I do know that later that day they went to have Christmas dinner at the home of some friends. Maybe they had ham or turkey and dressing with cranberries. The adults talked and the children played. They enjoyed Christmas Day with family and friends and planned to leave the next morning for Michigan.

Now here's what the accusers of John and Patsy Ramsey would have us believe:

That evening, these normal American parents took their children home, put their son to bed, fed their daughter some pineapple, changed her clothes. . .then sexually molested her, bashed her head with a baseball bat, strangled her with a rope and a stick, put duct tape on her mouth, covered her up, shut the door, wrote an absurd ransom not, went to bed, waited until morning, called the police and told them she had been kidnapped. What a ludicrous theory!

These intelligent people left the body IN their house and then called the police to COME to their house, *knowing* the house would be searched? *Why would they have done that*?

John could have said that they found the door open in the morning and that would have been a real clue that an outsider had done it. But John told the police the truth--that he thought all of the doors were locked. That made it look like no one could have gotten in. *Why would he have said that?*

We are asked to believe that the Ramseys wrote a ransom note saying someone would call--*knowing* that no one would ever call. *Why would they have done that?* Why not just say in the note, "We took your daughter and we are going to kill her?" That way, the police wouldn't hang around waiting for a phone call.

The killer left the pad of paper in the home with a practice ransom note inside it for the police to find. **Why would John have handed that pad to the police when they asked for something to write on? Wouldn't that be a stupid thing**

to do?

The killer left part of the stick that was used for the strangulation in Patsy's art supply box *knowing* that the police would search the house and probably find it there. **Why would Patsy have done that?**

And then, after they had supposedly committed this monstrous crime and left all sorts of clues around so they could be accused, Patsy and John just turned back into the normal people that they had always been. **How could they do that?**

Why not break a window? Why not insist the door was open? So simple. Why not get rid of the paper and the pen? Why not get rid of the body for that matter? Why call the police so early? They had time to get rid of things and call the police later, saying they woke up at 7 or 8 a.m. There is just nothing at all that makes sense about thinking they were involved!

The accusers would have us believe that John and Patsy both turned into monsters on the same ONE night of their lives. Never before and never since that night have either of these people shown any--any--indication of malice, of abusive tendencies, of crazy behavior, of strange thoughts. Not a hint. Not an instance. Nothing. But supposedly they BOTH became child abusers and murderers at exactly the same time. How could that happen? It couldn't.

Because if you believe one of them did it, then it seems like you must believe the other participated or at least covered up. Can you imagine covering up the murder of your own child? Of course not. Can you imagine Patsy saying, "Oh, John, I've just strangled JonBenét; can you help me move her body?" Can you imagine John saying, "Patsy, dear, I just accidentally killed JonBenét. Would you help me write a ransom note so that the police won't think I did it?"

The fact that they were BOTH home is even more proof they didn't do it because even if you could imagine that one person suddenly snapped, it's not even reasonable to believe that two normal people went insane at exactly the same time. That wouldn't even make good fiction.

The police say it's not logical that it was a stranger. I agree with them. No one just came in off of the street to do this. And if it was a stalker who preyed on little girls or was obsessed with JonBenét, how could he write this ransom note? The killer seemed to know too much. I think it had to be someone who knew the Ramseys.

In my opinion, the murderer obviously hated the Ramsey parents or was very jealous for some reason. Was it because John was successful and the killer was not? Did it have something to do with John's business? Was it because Patsy was pretty and well-loved and the killer was not? Was it because they had such a terrific family and the killer did not? It was just pure insanity--but in the warped mind of the killer, this was the way to hurt the Ramseys the most. The murderer left clues to be sure the police would come to the conclusion that the Ramseys had killed their daughter. This was the way to destroy the Ramseys. And the killer knew it.

To me, it was planned, it was brutal, it was no mistake, it had a purpose. And the purpose was not just to kill a little girl. The purpose was to hurt John or Patsy or both of them in a disgusting, insane way. Who could this have been? What was the real motivation? What was the sick reasoning of a sick mind?

We may never know. Because the police decided very shortly after this happened that John and Patsy were the prime suspects and it appears that the authorities NEVER SERIOUSLY LOOKED ANYWHERE ELSE! Although it makes me very angry, I don't think that the police did this with evil intentions. I am sad to say they probably thought they were doing the right thing. And that's what makes this so tragic. Their reasoning was that "most crimes like this are committed by the parents." Well, that's not good enough!

Sure, we all remember the Susan Smith case where a mother drowned her two children. We had all cried and prayed for Susan Smith. And we felt betrayed by Susan Smith when we heard the truth. I think that the public was angry and ready to blame the very next parents who found themselves in this position. But that's not fair!

Because we also know of parents who did NOT do it. We know about Adam Walsh's parents and about Polly Klaus's parents and there are hundreds more parents who have had their child murdered and they are completely innocent. But how many times has someone said, "It's usually the parents" and became suspicious of the innocent, grieving parents? And even if there are other parents who have been guilty, that is no excuse to jump to the conclusion that the next parent is guilty! We need to treat each case individually and each parent as a human being.

From the beginning the police made it clear that they suspected John and Patsy. And then they wondered why John and Patsy didn't want to talk to them any more. The police tried to keep their baby's body from being buried until they would submit to interrogation. Things were leaked to the press that seemed meant to pressure John and Patsy or to justify the police jumping to a conclusion. And much of the press played right into their hands by accepting these leaks and publishing what they were expected to. Were they really objective? Or were they also jumping to conclusions because they had only heard one side of the story?

Some television shows hired "professionals" to "analyze" the Ramseys. These people had never met Patsy or John and were not even involved with the case, but they had no hesitation to say terrible things about two wonderful human beings. It was like they just wanted to puff themselves up at the expense of someone else. Why do they think they have to destroy people to get ratings?

One talk show host who assumes he always has the right answer said, "If it was my child, I sure would talk to the police!" That's easy to say. Because, first of all, it wasn't your child. God forbid anyone would have something like this happen. You don't know what you would do!

But, if it did happen and you were innocent--and you were grieving--and you were in shock--and you were angry--then you would expect everyone to quickly move to find the guilty party. But what if the people who were supposed to find the killer were convinced *you* were guilty? What if they refused to seriously look elsewhere? Don't you see why you would be hurt and frustrated? Why would you submit yourself to people whose goal was to prove you had killed your baby?

As you can tell, even writing about this makes me very angry. It seems so logical to me that they were not involved. Nothing about it makes sense. And it seems so **il**logical that the police and the media don't spend more energy trying to find who really did it. It is so frustrating, but there is nothing we can do except to speak out.

And so we have done that. You have just read the heartfelt words of people from Patsy and John's past and present who are willing to stand beside them because they know them so well. And they know in their hearts and souls that Patsy and John could never hurt, let alone kill, their baby. These are good people who stand beside the Ramseys.

These friends and family members KNOW Patsy and John could not have done this. Just as you must know people who are not capable of such an act--just as you would bet all that you own that certain people you know could not do this--that is how certain Patsy and John's friends and family are that they are the victims of *two* horrible crimes. . .first, the murder of their daughter and then the false accusations that they were involved.

Sometimes I envy Patsy her unshakable faith. She believes that God is the Lord of her life and that somehow He will reveal a purpose from all of this tragedy and heartache.

I hope she is right.

Dear God,
When my child asks me why--
Why must I do this? Why can't I go there?
Why should I follow your will?
Sometimes I have to answer,
Because I am the mother, that's why.
My child may not understand now
But I know he will understand someday.
For now, he must learn to accept.

Dear God,
When I ask You why--
Why did You take them? Why must we suffer?
Why should I follow Your will?
Sometimes You have to answer,
Because I am the Father, that's why.
I may not understand now
But I pray You will let me understand someday.
For now, let me learn to accept.

Linda Edison McLean